"Nikolaj and Didde Flor Rotne offer a practical and straightforward guide to creating mindful learning environments, while helping ourselves in the process. With thought provoking science, case studies, and anecdotes, this book inspires and educates the reader."

—CHRISTOPHER WILLARD, *Child's Mind*

"The personal stories, case studies, and everyday practices presented in *Everybody Present* provide valuable inspiration for teachers who want to bring mindfulness into their classrooms and and into their lives. Snapshots of the teaching life are interwoven with concepts from Thich Nhat Hanh and findings from recent brain research to inform a mindful approach to teaching and learning in today's world."

—IRENE McHENRY, PhD., Executive Director,
    Friends Council on Education

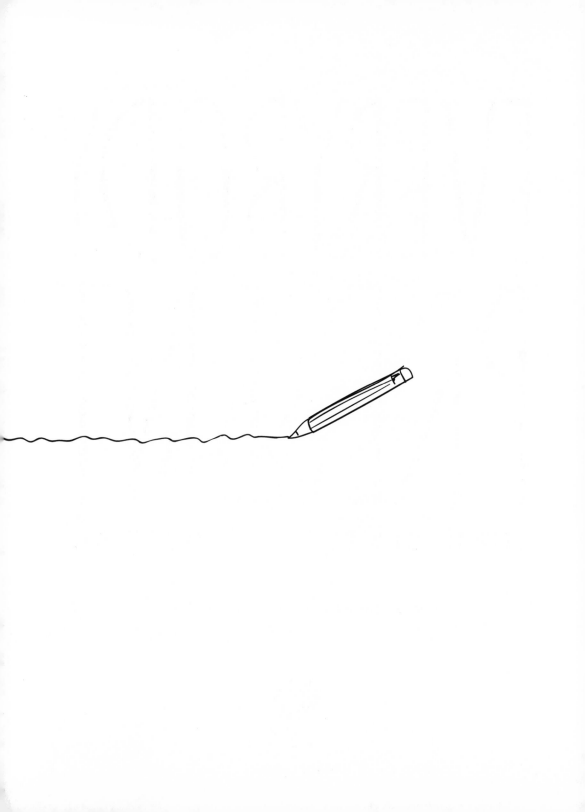

EVERYBODY PRESENT

MINDFULNESS IN EDUCATION

Nikolaj Flor Rotne and Didde Flor Rotne

PARALLAX
PRESS

Berkeley, California

Parallax Press
P.O. Box 7355
Berkeley, California 94707

Parallax Press is the publishing division of
Unified Buddhist Church, Inc.

Translated by Peter Snow
Cover and text design by Debbie Berne
Illustrations © Wietske Vriezen

Printed on recycled paper

Library of Congress Cataloging-in-Publication Data
is available upon request.

1 2 3 4 5 / 17 16 15 14 13

*Dedicated with grateful thanks to
Thich Nhat Hanh and Valentin,
Leonard, and Johannes*

Strawberry blossoms
catch the hare in their wild light
nothing is hidden

DIDDE FLOR ROTNE

Contents

A New Approach to Education

OUR CHILDREN ARE OUR DEAREST TREASURES. They are the future's gold and society's greatest resource. Assuring a beautiful future requires that we offer all our children a good education. Children need to be well-educated to create a world in which every single person is able to flourish and take responsibility for his or her own well-being and that of others, to create a world characterized by interconnectedness, awareness, and joy.

In December 2012, during the writing of this book, twenty children and six staff members were killed in a school shooting at Sandy Hook Elementary School in Newtown, Connecticut. How could something so incomprehensible happen? What caused a twenty-year-old man to commit this massacre? A crime with such traumatic consequences demands great insight and the ability to look deeply into the situation before it can really be understood. One answer comes from the thirty-seven-year-old Zen monk Thay Phap Luu, who lives in Plum Village, in France. He grew up in Newtown and lived near Sandy Hook school as a child. After the tragedy, he wrote a letter to the perpetrator that was shared through social media. In his letter, Phap Luu wrote:

> As a community we need to sit down and learn how to cherish life, not with gun-checks and security, but by

being fully present for one another, by being truly there
for one another.

But how do we do that in practice? How can we learn to be fully present for each other?

All children experience some degree of stress and alienation. We know that the happier and healthier children are, the easier they learn. We tell our students that they should pay attention and be kind, but can we show them how to do it?

Mindfulness means to be aware of what is happening in our present experiences, with compassion, insight, and an intention to create joy. With mindfulness, compassion, insight, and joy arise very naturally. Mindfulness practice can bring a change in our approach to teaching and provide the kind of nurturing our children need. Teachers and parents can lead the way by training ourselves to live in mindfulness. Then we can teach children mindfulness through our own life and practice.

Mindfulness helps us to:
- Strengthen inner peace and prevent stress
- Sharpen our senses and see clearly what is happening in and around us
- Avoid falling into the grip of emotions and reacting unconsciously or out of habit
- Concentrate and be free of the tyranny of thoughts
- Support contagious joy and an ethic of altruism
- Better understand our students and create a good learning environment
- Help children become wiser, friendlier, calmer, and more joyful

Mindfulness helps establish a learning culture that facilitates social and personal development. Mindfulness teaches us to be fully present for ourselves and for others. The practice gives teachers the ability to anchor themselves in their profession with greater inner peace, openness, and insight; from this starting point they can create a more harmonious and fruitful learning environment.

In the book *A Mindful Nation*, Congressman Tim Ryan gives many examples of schools in the United States that have had great success in implementing secular mindfulness practices in the classroom. *Everybody Present* comes out of our wish to give educators a practical guidebook to the practice of mindfulness. The book offers basic knowledge and insight into the many benefits mindfulness has to offer. The word "teacher" is used throughout as a catchall term for anyone working in the field of education. Although this book is primarily written for teachers and education professionals, it's also intended for anyone who works in education or has an interest in teaching and raising children, including parents, teacher's aides, and those training to be teachers.

We hope to demonstrate how an individual's inner peace is the basis for experiencing interbeing, an awareness of the interconnectedness and interdependence of all things in the world. This state of awareness can change an underlying feeling of inadequacy to one of abundance, confidence, and well-being. Teachers will benefit from this feeling of abundance, and this will create an ever-stronger culture of mindfulness that can nourish coming generations, beginning in their most formative years.

Everybody Present aims to give the reader a nuanced experience and understanding of mindfulness, with an emphasis on incorporating mindfulness practice on a daily basis in educational settings. In order to demonstrate more vividly the fruits of mindfulness practice, we've included a number of stories that may bring additional insights and ideas. It's our hope that this book will give you a foundation for your own mindfulness practice, so that you can more effectively teach it to others. We've included a number of exercises that are concrete and accessible. We've also developed an accompanying eWorkbook to support teachers in beginning and cultivating a personal mindfulness practice. It consists of a twenty-one-day mindfulness program for teachers called *Inner Peace and Contagious Happiness for Education's Superstars*. You can download the eWorkbook at www.stillnessrevolution.com

We would very much like to thank Thich Nhat Hanh, Jon Kabat-Zinn, Tim Ryan, Jack Kornfield, David Loy, Tara Brach, Daniel Goleman, Richard Davidson, Shauna Shapiro and Linda Carlson, Barbara Frederickson, Susan Kaiser Greenland, and Christopher Willard for their inspiration. A special thank you to Peter Snow and to Rachel Neumann for making this book available in English, as well as to Søren Bogø, Martin Ammentorp, and Dorthe Møller for their written contributions to this book.

Nikolaj Flor Rotne and Didde Flor Rotne
Denmark, 2013.

CHAPTER 1

Combining Personal and Social Change

IN NOVEMBER 1998, WE TRAVELED TO SCOTLAND, to revisit the beautiful country where Didde had lived for three years as a teenager while attending the Waldorf school in Edinburgh. On our journey, we visited the little west coast island of Iona, in the Hebrides. Iona is known for having a very thin veil between sky and sea. During our stay, we clearly observed sky and sea becoming one. That stormy autumn, the foamy waves beat against the rocks, and mist and rain wiped out the horizon. There is an old abbey on the island, founded in 563 BCE by the Irish monk Columba. In that period, the abbey was the center for the spread of Christianity in Scotland. Today the abbey is the setting for an interchurch, ecumenical movement. In the abbey bookshop we found the book *Living Buddha, Living Christ* by the Zen teacher Thich Nhat Hanh. The back cover text and the photo of the monk, at once strong and gentle-looking, made a profound impression on us. That was our first introduction to mindfulness.

The following year we encountered mindfulness again when we read Thich Nhat Hanh's *Peace Is Every Step*. This poetic little book is filled with daily exercises in mindfulness, and it shows how peace within ourselves is a precondition for peace in the world. We were so taken up with his mindfulness philosophy that we resolved to take a journey. We gave up our lease, put our few belongings into storage, and quit our jobs. Our journey led us, among other places, to Plum

Village, Thich Nhat Hanh's community in southwest France. During our stay, we had many revelations. We saw how it was possible, in a down-to-earth way, to try to solve social and existential challenges. In the community we learned a way to build up our own inner peace and contentment, combined with engagement in society and the impetus to make the world better.

In our meeting with Thich Nhat Hanh, who is now eighty-six, we discovered a mindfulness practice that impressed us in its ease and simplicity. At Plum Village, each individual works first on her own challenges and on striving to be the change she wishes to see in the world. The culture there is based on being fully present in the moment, and it produced in us a deep feeling of interbeing—an experience of belonging and of feeling at home in the world. We could observe the strength of mindfulness both as an individual practice and as a group practice.

When we returned to Denmark three months later, we had nowhere to live, no money, no formal training, and no jobs. We couch-surfed at our friends' homes. One late summer evening, we found ourselves sitting on a bench in Copenhagen. It was almost sunset and we didn't know where we were going to spend the night. We had nothing apart from each other, but we'd discovered the most important thing: the practice of mindfulness. Mindfulness practice became our basis for creating a family and for ongoing field of research during our studies—in teacher-training college for both of us and thereafter for Nikolaj in postgraduate studies in educational psychology. Mindfulness became the foundation for our working lives. We also went on to research mindfulness from a theoretical approach. We wanted to understand the science behind mindfulness and to research the possibilities of mindfulness practice in the educational environment.

The Intention to Practice Mindfulness

When we came home from our course in Plum Village in the summer of 2000, mindfulness was virtually unknown Denmark. Today mindfulness has found its way into many aspects of social and personal life. Research shows that there are many reasons to practice mindfulness and that such intentions themselves can change for those practicing it. We've divided the intentions behind meditation practices into four phases: 1) self-regulation, 2) self-examination, 3) self-transcendence, and 4) selfless service (Shapiro 1992).

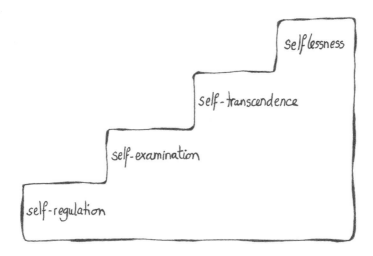

FIGURE 1:1. This four-step model shows how the practitioner's abilities and experiences evolve to new phases.

1. *Self-regulation.* Many of us who embark upon mindfulness practice are seeking mastery over ourselves. We look for inner calm and tranquility in a stressful daily life. We may use mindfulness as a stepping stone to personal growth, or as a source of help if we are stressed out at work, or perhaps

because we're seeking relief from circular thinking. Self-regulation is our primary goal in this first phase.

2. *Self-examination.* We wish to gradually become more self-aware, and we use mindfulness as a way to explore our inner world. We examine ourselves to try to understand the relationships that allow for more success in everyday life and in the workplace.

3. *Self-transcendence.* As our mindfulness practice evolves, we try to go beyond the sense of the self as a separate entity, and we experience the feeling that we are a part of our surroundings, that we belong to the world. This experience brings with it a heightened sense of responsibility, not just for ourself, but also for whatever situation or context we enter into. This reinforces the sensation of belonging, which we might call interbeing. This phase is the starting point of our experience of self-transcendence.

4. *Selflessness.* Ultimately, helping others and helping restore balance to the planet are essential parts of our mindfulness practice. Our own happiness and sorrows are woven in with those of others. Selfless service becomes our primary motivation.

There is a strong focus in the Western world on the self. Independence and autonomy are seen as virtues, as are self-esteem, healthy boundaries, and the discovery of our own unique potential. Mindfulness is popularly used as a path to self-discipline and stress management. Of course, self-esteem and knowing one's needs and limitations are positive things that are directly related to self-regulation and self-examination. But focusing exclusively on the self can lead us to overlook the sufferings of others and miss out on the deep joy that comes from transcending the experience of the self. Albert Einstein beautifully described the transition from self-examination to self-transcendence:

> A person is part of the wholeness that we call the universe, a part that is limited in time and space. He experiences himself, his thoughts and feelings as something separate from the rest . . . a kind of optical illusion of the consciousness. This illusion is a kind of prison for us that limits us to our personal desires and affections for some few people close to us. Our task must be to liberate ourselves from this prison by broadening our compassion to encompass all living beings and all of nature in its beauty (Einstein 2000).

The deepening of phase 3 (self-transcendence) and phase 4 (selflessness) show the nuanced possibilities that mindfulness offers us and explains why we may be motivated to begin a mindfulness practice or intensify an existing practice. While we may not have "arrived" at self-transcendence and selflessness, we can keep these ideas in mind as our ultimate intention and direction.

CHAPTER 2
What Is Mindfulness?

MINDFULNESS IS A UNIVERSAL HUMAN CAPACITY that is accessible to everyone. Originating in Buddhist philosophy and psychology, mindfulness embraces a way of being present in the world. It's a scientific term, as opposed to terms like *conscious presence* or *joyous attentiveness*.

Mindfulness means to be aware of what is happening in our present experiences, observing with compassion, insight, and an intention to create joy.

Mindfulness practice can be seen overall as an intentional, systematic way of developing a compassionate and insightful presence in the world. There are formal and informal mindfulness practices. Formal practice involves regular exercises while we're sitting or walking that can be incorporated into daily life as simple, short meditations. We may explore these meditations more profoundly at immersion retreats where we can gain a greater understanding of the practice and learn new habits.

Informal practice refers to the use of mindfulness in daily life, where we establish an attentive presence while performing daily activities such as cooking, conversing, and using the computer. Mindfulness practice is based on attentiveness to breathing. This process makes us aware of the subjective and transient nature of our thoughts and feelings, rather than regarding them as permanent and valid. We begin to understand that our thoughts aren't necessarily truths, and that thoughts come and go. Often our preconceptions about a colleague, parent, or child stand in the way of our working well together because we don't look deeply at the spontaneous judgment or hostility we feel. Then it dawns on us that the person we're judging is actually quite different from our initial perceptions. Mindfulness practice can help us steer clear of the judgments that cloud our interactions with others.

Intention, Attentiveness, and Attitude

Three concepts form the backbone of our mindfulness practice:

1. Intention
2. Attentiveness
3. Attitude

(Shapiro and Carlson 2009)

Intention is the direction we have for our practice. In mindfulness the overall direction is to create more happiness and less suffering for ourselves and others. There are two kinds of happiness: *hedonism* and *eudaimonia*. Hedonism is built on the notion that pleasure creates happiness. This happiness is temporary and primarily centered around our desires being satisfied. Eudaimonia—the happiness that mindfulness practice brings—is the happiness we experience when we feel connected to other people. This is the kind of happiness that makes us flourish.

So there's an ethical dimension to mindfulness. When you buy an ice cream cone, you're satisfying hedonistic happiness. When a teacher wishes to demonstrate eudaimonic happiness, she can model it with her own helpful behavior. She might also offer an exercise which allows students to experience the joy of helping others or of working together on a project.

Intention isn't an aspiration making us forget the now in favor of dreams we have for the future. Intention is a motivation connected with the now.

Attentiveness refers to a method of sharpening our attention, giving us a clear view of what's going on in the present moment. Unstable attention is like an unstable camera—the picture is blurred. Mindfulness practice is based on—through attentiveness to our breathing—accepting the thoughts and perceptions that come to our attention, regardless of their nature. This brings focus and inner calm. There are two types of attentiveness: focused attentiveness is directed toward a chosen object (like when we count our breaths); and open, receptive attentiveness registers whatever comes and goes. Both are exercised in mindfulness practice.

Attitude is the manner in which we relate to whatever comes to our attention. It's important that we have an attitude of compassion and acceptance. We recognize that there can be several perspectives on a particular matter, or on our own thoughts. We also refrain from identifying with the thoughts and emotions that arise in the moment. That is how we learn that we're neither the thoughts in our brain, nor the feelings that can be so overpowering.

Decentering and Disidentification

Two other important concepts that inform our mindfulness practice are *decentering* and *disidentification*. Decentering refers to the idea of observing something without identifying with it (Covey 2005). Traditionally, many of us observe the world through the filter of how it affects us and our own situations. For instance, when we become annoyed with a parent for perhaps arriving late for the second time in a week to pick up her daughter, our attentiveness can be full of thoughts that revolve around this parent's irresponsible and disrespectful behavior. Practicing decentering gives us the possibility to observe our thoughts, feelings, and sensations as they play themselves out, without being controlled by them. It allows us to step out of our mental dramas and bear witness in a nonjudgmental manner. Instead of meeting this parent seething with irritation, we can discuss the parent's conduct in a calm and peaceful way and see if we can help with the underlying causes. Decentering allows us to choose consciously how we want to respond to external stimuli.

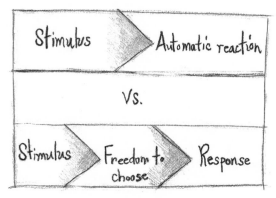

FIGURE 1.2 Automatic reaction vs. Conscious response (Decentering)

Disidentification is a key part of decentering. Practicing disidentification allows our thoughts, feelings, and sense impressions to be there, without identifying ourselves with them. If you and a colleague disagree about something, say whether students in the middle grades should remain inside during recess, the discussion can develop into a long personal battle in which each participant identifies strongly with their own opinion. Once we've engaged in battle, we all have the tendency to keep fighting because we think there's something that needs to be won. It can become very difficult to hear what the other person is saying when you're so taken up with forcing through your own point of view. When you disidentify, you find that your opinions, thoughts, and feelings around a given situation do not threaten your own self-image,

Mindfulness Exercise
BREATH

The following mindfulness exercise takes only five minutes and puts the concepts of *intention*, *attentiveness*, and *attitude* into practice.

Sit with a straight back and have the intention to create joy. Observe your in-breath and out-breath with an attitude of compassionate attentiveness. Place your hand on your stomach so you can notice your breathing. Observe what arises in your awareness with an attitude of acceptance. Smile and return to your awareness of your breathing.

and the discussion can be a meaningful, productive exchange of views that leads to a good result for the middle graders, for example, without losing a friendship over it. Teachers who practice these techniques as part of their mindfulness practice report that the techniques enable them to be more effective in conflict situations. They become better at listening to others and more aware of new possibilities for learning (Miller 2006; Solloway 1999).

Mindfulness and Insight

Mindfulness practice brings to our lives a series of greater insights. As we practice being attentive we're able to see ourselves more and more as part of a context, and we identify with our own thoughts and emotions less and less. Identifying with our thoughts and emotions creates a sense of separation from the world. Mindfulness practice facilitates a greater sense of connection to the world. This in turn brings us happiness and a greater sense of responsibility. Through continuous practice we build a mindful presence, gradually changing our way of being in the world.

As teachers we often focus primarily on going through the syllabus. Mindfulness makes us more aware of how our own way of being affects the children. The practice creates the opportunity to live life *off* autopilot and not avoid the things we'd rather not see. Mindfulness also gives us new insights into how we deal with anger, desire, and habitual thinking. We realize that these mental states breed emotional suffering and a lack of clarity. Through mindfulness we develop the ability to see more clearly the effects of anger on ourselves and others, and we learn to say yes or no without irritation. These insights will gradually become more and more integrated in our mindfulness practice and strengthen our potential for conducting ourselves in a manner that reduces suffering and promotes happiness.

CHAPTER 3
Rediscovering Our Educational Ideals

TEACHERS ARE THE MOST IMPORTANT PROFESSIONAL RESOURCE children have for learning, growth, and development. But many teachers suffer from chronic stress on account of a tense work environment and feelings of inadequacy. In spite of the fact that teachers are so crucial for the well-being and prosperity of the next generation, the teaching profession has neither the status, nor the opportunities equal to the expectations placed on teachers.

Most teachers crave an excellent teaching environment and the opportunity to create a culture of learning. If we want teachers to have stability and good health, and if we want to increase learning and growth for the next generation, we need a new direction. Mindfulness practice shows a new way to increase teachers' happiness and professional outlook by strengthening their inner calm and competence.

Many people who work in education and vocational training have high ideals. Most teachers have chosen their profession in part to show the next generation a path toward a good future. This attitude creates the necessary engagement and vision for their work. At the same time, many teachers have the feeling that they are forever behind and underachieving because it's hard for them to live up to their ideals. A teacher's ideals often go hand in hand with a sense of personal responsibility: the feeling that whether we succeed or fail is completely up to us. This means that we constantly feel we're lacking something; that we could and should be doing better, and that it's our duty to find a way to improve the situation. This can lead to a permanent sense of inadequacy, in which nothing we do is ever good enough, coupled with the feeling that it's all our own fault.

Soon the glow of our idealism is dimmed by stress and the feeling that we just don't measure up. The daily demands of teaching are such that we rarely get time to spend with each child every day. This also weighs on our conscience, producing a chronic sense of inadequacy. Over and over, we go home at the end of each day feeling that we just didn't do enough: "Oh, no! I didn't get time to give Jeremy extra help with reading today," or "I didn't handle the conflict between Keisha and Anna very effectively."

Mindfulness offers us a way to reconnect with the ideals that led us into the educational profession in the first place. Some may worry that mindfulness could become yet another ideal that's hard to live up to. First, the right conditions should be created for the practice of mindfulness in educational culture, so that no individual feels it's her sole responsibility to improve the educational situation. We aren't the sole authors of our own happiness; human beings live within a network of reciprocal influence. Our surroundings, our genetic heritage, the culture we were raised in and live in all affect us and the people we work with. We need to do what we can to improve the educational environment, and at the same time be gentle in our understanding of ourselves and others.

Secondly, mindfulness means focusing on appreciating each new moment before we begin to anticipate what the future may bring. It offers us abundance in the present moment and makes us more creative in imagining the kind of future we'd like to have. This helps us to bring the challenges of realizing our highest ideals within the scope of everyday life, so that we're not forever trying to keep up, but are happy within the present moment, while at the same time we're cocreating a better future. *Everybody Present* shows us a path to fulfilling our ideals without being crushed by them. The practice of mindfulness can help us to rediscover our ideals and refresh ourselves and our careers.

The following story, *The Circle of Ninety-Nine,* illustrates the constant sense of inadequacy many teachers may feel.

The Circle of Ninety-Nine

Once upon a time there was an unhappy king who had a cheerful and helpful servant. The king wished to know why the servant was always so happy, so he summoned his counselor. The counselor told the king it was because the servant was outside the Circle of Ninety-Nine. He offered to show the king how the circle worked, but it would come at a cost: the king would have to be willing to lose his peerless servant. The king consented, and at the counselor's request, sent for a leather purse containing ninety-nine gold coins.

That night the king and the counselor met outside the servant's house. The counselor tied a message to the leather purse with these words on it: *This treasure is thine. It is payment for being a good man. Take it, but tell nobody how thou hast come upon it.* They tied the purse to the door, knocked, and hid themselves. When the servant found the purse, he emptied it out on the table. He had never held a gold coin before, and he played with them and caressed them. Finally, he began to count them, stacking the coins in piles of ten. One pile of ten, two piles, three piles, four, five, six . . . until he'd made the last pile— but there were only nine coins! That can't be right, he thought. He pushed the last pile up beside the others, and made sure that it was indeed smaller. "I've been robbed!" he cried. "Ninety-nine isn't a full count. A hundred is a full count."

The servant began to worry about how he could save enough to make up what he was lacking. In the end, he reckoned it would take him and his wife seven years, if they worked extra hard, to earn enough to equal one gold coin. The servant had been lured into the Circle of Ninety-Nine. It was not long before the servant was dismissed. It's not at all pleasant to have a servant about the place who's always in a bad mood. (Freely retold from Bucay 2013.)

The tale shows how we always feel we're short of something that could make us completely happy; if only we had that thing, we would be content. A seeming lack and a sense of separation are examples of things that can obstruct our way to deep and lasting happiness. We want to formulate a different way of being, a state in which there's no lack, in which ninety-nine coins make up a hundred percent of the treasure.

When we experience ourselves as separate from our surroundings, we'll always feel that something is lacking. But if we can escape from the illusion that we're separate from everyone and everything, we can develop a sense of abundance that helps us to complete our tasks effectively, set goals for the future, and make a contribution to the next generation.

CHAPTER 4
From Vicious Circle to Virtuous Circle

WHEN WE THINK OF OURSELVES as disconnected and separate, we may find ourselves in a constant state of lacking something (Loy 2000). To avoid the discomfort of this feeling, we may resort to a range of distractions, from alcohol and food, to television and compulsive shopping, to an excessive craving for acknowledgment. When these diversions fail to satisfy us, we may be overwhelmed by negative emotions such as anger, loneliness, and inadequacy. Underneath it all is a great longing for the experience of interbeing: the sense of belonging and connection to the world.

Mindfulness practice can open and enhance our capacity for interbeing. Mindfulness practice sharpens our senses and strengthens our ability to interact on the basis of presence and appreciation. Understanding others takes time and attentiveness. It requires the courage to be silent and sensitive to what's going on in ourselves, in others, and in the space between. When we begin to listen and be attentive to what takes place in the moment with an attitude of acceptance and the intention to promote happiness, we cultivate the capacity for interbeing and presence.

The following diagram of two circles illustrates how these mechanisms work on each other. The practice of mindfulness offers us the possibility of moving from the vicious circle to the virtuous circle. The vicious circle is made up of *unconsciousness, alienation,* and *dissatisfaction.*

The three attitudes exacerbate each other. When we are unconscious, we are reactive and behave out of established habits. We're not free in our choices and hence often in the grip of our thoughts and feelings. We're unconscious of our rootedness in the world, and so we feel alienated. The experience of alienation creates a fundamental attitude of loss, estrangement, and dissatisfaction. Dissatisfaction and isolation reinforce the vicious circle of self-centeredness. How do we break out of the vicious circle?

Mindfulness Is the Stepping Stone

Mindfulness practice is the stepping stone that allows us to put the negative circle behind us and evolve to a fundamentally new way of being in the world. The virtuous circle is composed of *consciousness, interbeing*, and *joy*. Through mindfulness practice, we're fully conscious of what is happening inside us and around us. We learn how to respond consciously to things that arise in our awareness, without reacting automatically from the grip of our thoughts or feelings. We're free to choose our way of acting and responding. This gives us the possibility to further our own and others' joy and sense of interbeing. The joy we speak of here is the eudaimonic joy: a profound joy that fosters the experience of interbeing. Research shows that the more positive feelings we have for another person, the greater the sense of interbeing we have with that person.

One part of the work of interbeing consists in finding out what we have in common with others. The feeling of interbeing is a driving force in helping others in need (Cialdini et al. 1997). This means that we're willing to an ever-greater degree to help those with whom we feel a kinship, which again increases joy. Positive feelings and compassion create both joy and interbeing. Studies have proven that there is a greater probability that people who are feeling good will be kind

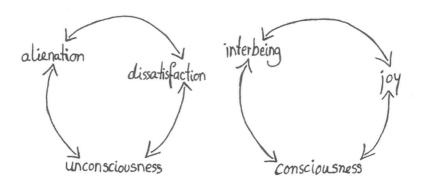

FIGURE 2:1. The vicious circle on the left shows how *unconsciousness, alienation*, and *dissatisfaction* work together in a negative way. The circle on the right shows the virtuous circle: *consciousness, interbeing, and joy*. The arrows show the areas that particularly reinforce their mutual connections.

and offer help to strangers (Isen 1972, 1976, 1987). In the same way, emotional balance fosters greater selflessness when it comes to helping others (Batson 2002, Eisenberg 2002).

Positive Feelings Expand Awareness

Positive relationships play a determining role in the world of child and adult education. Positive emotions help to expand our awareness so we can take in more information about ourselves and the world. This is known as the "broaden and build" theory; it shows that positivity makes us more creative and open to many possibilities (Frederickson 1998, 2010).

The same theory shows that positivity brings out the best in us, physically, psychologically, and socially, through increased feelings of interbeing and helpfulness. Interbeing gives us peace of mind, diminishes inappropriate defense mechanisms, and erases our need to assert ourselves at the expense of others. As teachers, there are considerable benefits to finding areas of interbeing with children, parents, and colleagues, as well as building up relationships on a positive basis. In light of this, it's essential that we create learning environments that preserve and foster positivity and experiences of interbeing.

When we're busy helping others, we often forget to take care of ourselves at the same time. It's essential to build up our own inner peace, joy, and abundance to form a solid foundation from which to teach the younger generation inner peace, lasting joy, and compassion. When we're overworked and overcommitted, it is difficult to be fully present for the children. That feeling of "lacking something" leads to dissatisfaction, mistakes, and nagging. But even when we feel pressured, we can still learn to offer our presence, and in that way improve the outcomes for our students.

CHAPTER 5
Mindfulness as Educational Practice

IMAGINE YOU HAVE A CHILD IN YOUR CLASS WE'LL CALL JANE. Because of her behavior, she's not one of your favorite students. She's restless and has trouble making eye contact. It's difficult to establish a connection with her since she always seems to be on her way to the next place, person, or activity.

You suspect that the interaction between Jane and her parents is probably lacking true contact and care. You get the impression that Jane goes out of her way to avoid adults, and you yourself have had a series of negative experiences with her. She doesn't seem to pay attention to instructions given to the group and she frequently doesn't comply with polite requests such as being asked to wash her hands or put down her book. You're fed up with repeating yourself constantly and disturbed by the turbulence that always seems to surround her. Filled with irritation, you find yourself all too often yelling at Jane and generally speaking to her in a negative tone. How can you change this undesirable pattern?

In order to establish a positive and meaningful connection with Jane, it's crucial that you, as the teacher, display both generosity and calm in your encounters with her. Through mindfulness practice you can build up your inner calm and your ability to meet Jane without the negative, prejudiced assumptions you have accumulated. Being calm and having the intention to promote joy means you have something to offer her, and Jane will feel this and respond to it. Instead of no actual connection ever taking place, you're now building a foundation for the interaction to happen. You're making room for open-minded relations by demonstrating real interest in Jane and by displaying positive emotions.

In order to meet Jane with generosity and calm, you need to establish a basic mindfulness practice beforehand. Through attentiveness to breathing, you develop the ability to calm yourself, to avoid acting solely on your emotions and to see beyond Jane's unappealing aspects. You watch your breathing and remain aware of what happens inside and around you, observing without forming an opinion. If Jane annoys you, you acknowledge that you feel annoyed. You don't try to suppress or change the feeling; you just accept that this is what you feel. Acceptance will take care of the emotion. In acceptance, one is present with the difficult emotions.

Your basic mindfulness practice helps you gain mastery of yourself and remain present in your experience. Again and again, and with an attitude of kind determination, you direct your attention back to your breathing, which is your anchor to the present moment. This work is an internal practice that you do while you're interacting with Jane. All along, you remind yourself of your intention to reduce suffering and promote happiness.

Jane will slowly adjust to the new premise of your relationship. Gradually, a connection will develop. You help the process along by taking an interest in her ideas, establishing boundaries by presenting alternatives when necessary, and recognizing when she makes an effort.

When Jane challenges you, you return your focus to your breathing. Attentiveness to breathing settles your difficult emotions and brings about renewed energy to meet Jane with an appropriate disposition and commitment. Mindfulness practice creates the underlying inner calm, presence, and energy you need to make a positive connection with Jane, and with every other student.

The cultural challenges of today make tough demands on education. Amid the fast pace, information overflow, and numerous choices, mindfulness provides a space for silence and presence. This encourages a cultural change in schools and kindergartens, in which the human need for these qualities is recognized and integrated into daily life. Changing habits takes time, and mindfulness isn't a quick fix; rather it's a profound practice that can create profound changes.

Agents of Change

The ability to picture scenarios for the future is an amazing human capacity. This capacity is especially important in the field of education, since the teacher is helping the child develop her ambitions for the future. This makes the teacher an agent of change. What mindfulness imparts for this purpose is happiness and professional perspective by strengthening the teacher's inner calm, her powers of relating, and her ability to make qualified decisions, both professionally and personally. Studies show that teacher competence in the areas of relational skills and classroom management is the single most influential factor in a student's learning (Hattie 2009 and Nordenbo 2008).

Many teachers are keenly interested in exploring ways to strengthen learning environments and encourage positive interaction between themselves and their students. It's essential for a teacher's work that she be able to assert herself as an authority. Lack of authority fundamentally undermines the teacher's relationship with her students. Assuming authority in a positive manner is a prerequisite for any educational endeavor.

Understanding the Child and Taking Responsibility
for the Situation

Empathizing with children like Jane helps us understand why they behave the way they do. This brings us closer to their perception of reality, their motivations, and values. When we feel challenged by a child, it can be difficult to understand the child's intentions, and we may be inclined to see the child as the *problem*. In a situation like this, mindfulness practice can help us create inner calm and focus. This opens up our ability to absorb information in a way that doesn't maintain those difficult emotions that may cause us to misunderstand Jane. Empathy helps break through the deadlock and create awareness of new and more constructive courses of action. This helps us to retain responsibility for the quality of our relationships with our students.

A successful teacher-student connection requires that we're able to cope with and take responsibility for what arises, accepting the emotions and moods of a situation without assuming the emotions and moods of others. It's appropriate to make an effort to distinguish between the child and the child's behavior. The two aren't the same. The exercise is to always recognize someone as a person, without necessarily accepting her behavior. If one pupil hits a classmate, we still recognize her as a person, while in no way condoning her behavior. This distinction may prevent both unnecessary scolding and falling into the trap of overcontaining, with the invasion of our personal space as a consequence. We should use our insight to establish suitable boundaries. We may tell the child to stop her inappropriate behavior, but in a way that doesn't continue the mutual transference of negative emotions and motives. We use the language of "I" rather than the accusing "you." At the same time, we try to distinguish our own experience from that of others. If boundaries aren't established, if we're annoyed or feeling impotent, our professional relationship with the child will wither away. The child will lack confidence because she can't depend on her teacher.

Mindfulness helps the teacher handle a situation by maintaining the compassion and inner calm that enables a clear view of the context. When we empathize with someone and try to understand the logic and assumptions behind her behavior, we may ask ourselves: "What is she trying to achieve? What are her needs?"

Reflecting on the Learning Environment

In the field of education it's important to relate the child's behavior to the setting in which it takes place. Some teachers may feel defensive and a bit vulnerable when asked to examine their own practice. This may be because teachers by definition work with a part of their own self invested in the process, and therefore may feel challenged, not just professionally but personally.

As a teacher, one is embedded in and cocreator of a reciprocal practice community. When a problem arises in the educational environment, it may result from something that needs to be changed or strengthened in the teacher's own habits and techniques. Many teachers wish to find a new perspective on how they prepare and go about their work. Mindfulness creates the clarity and calm we need to examine our own practice objectively so that we may reflect more clearly on it. Here, a question such as: "How does my practice and the learning environment affect my students?" is pivotal.

During the writing of this book, we observed several different teachers begin their lessons. One young fourth-grade teacher came to class carrying a brown leather briefcase with a handle. Every morning when the bell rang, he let go of the handle, dropping the bag on the floor. It made a resounding smack on the floor: The lesson had begun! The scene was set—and so was the mood! We couldn't resist smiling, because it seemed so funny to begin the day and the lesson with such an "impact." From our point of view, this wasn't a good way to create a secure learning environment. One of the best first impressions we observed was a teacher who greeted each student individually at the beginning of class, giving each child a warm handshake and making eye contact. In this way, the teacher set the scene and created confidence and calm before the lesson began.

The Boy Under the Oak

A boy was sitting under a beautiful old oak. He was enjoying nature and feeling very good, yet he thought: "Wouldn't it be nice to have a small cabin and a bed to nap on?" And before he knew it, a small wooden cabin had emerged next to the tree. The boy entered the cabin. There was a freshly made bed, and with a smile the boy lay down to rest. Later, he awoke with a feeling of contentment. He yawned and stretched and thought: "A good meal would be nice right now." And before he knew it, he was surrounded by the delicious aromas of all his favorite dishes. The boy ate with relish until he was pleasantly full. He was feeling very good indeed and then thought it might be nice to have someone to play with. Before he knew it, he found himself among his friends playing. After having played a while, he started pondering the strangeness of having all his wishes granted. Could the old oak be enchanted? Maybe a demon lived in the tree? Before he knew it, a demon appeared among the branches. "Hello there!" the boy said. And he thought: "I wonder if the demon is good or evil? I bet it's evil. I'm afraid it'll eat me." And the demon did. (Adapted from Willard 2010).

This story of the boy under the oak illustrates how our thoughts help to create our reality. Applying this principle to the educational world, we realize that it's essential to have a clear idea of the direction of our professional endeavors. Research shows that students will generally meet their teacher's expectations (Rosenthal 2002). When a teacher expects a student to do well, she's more likely to smile at him and praise him. This explanation is supported by studies showing that the more positive a learning environment is, the greater academic success the student is likely to achieve (Harris and Rosenthal 1985).

The following section provides two examples of a focus that facilitates positivity in educational culture: opportunity before obstacles and today before tomorrow.

Opportunity before Obstacles

If we choose to see the opportunities before the obstacles, we're rewarded with hope, ease, and the motivation to overcome challenges. For instance, Lana is picking up her son Michael from kindergarten. Michael's friend wants to continue their friendly wrestling and therefore is trying to pull Michael back while Lana is juggling clothes, shoes, and bags and at the same time trying to talk to the kindergarten teacher. Lana may choose to focus on the problem—the bothersome behavior—or she can offer Michael new opportunities, and ask him what game he might like to play right now.

The circle of influence is a tool we can use to maintain this kind of perspective. The inner circle of the figure represents the potential for influence, and the outer circle represents everything that's outside our influence in a given situation and that therefore might cause futile speculations. Rather than assuming the role of victim or complaining about matters beyond our control, we focus on what we can influence and act upon the area of opportunity in the center of the circle of

41

influence. This is where our focus should be (Covey 2005). When we allow ourselves to become aware of our feelings, thoughts, or physical sensations, we gain the capacity to act and live in harmony with what *is*.

We may not always know where our opportunities for influence lie. In searching for those opportunities, we can turn to the classic serenity prayer:

Grant me the serenity to accept the things I cannot change,
The courage to change the things I can,
And the wisdom to know the difference.

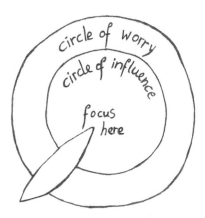

FIGURE 2:2. The circle of worry illustrates the area that's worrying us, but that's beyond our control. Within that, the arrow points to an area where there's opportunity for action, the circle of influence (Covey 2005).

Today before Tomorrow

Accepting the present moment, with all the frustrations, insecurity, and uncertainty it may hold, is a cornerstone in all mindfulness practices. Appreciating the present moment is sometimes a challenge. We may be so busy pursuing future goals or being frustrated about things we wish to avoid that we completely miss the present moment, which is where the opportunities for happiness and influence lie. We must "bring the present moment home." When the present moment is a difficult one, remaining in it and accepting it can be a great challenge. In order to change this difficult present moment, it's necessary to face the reality of it and accept things as they are. Not until we accept what is can we start to change it. If you look the ogre in the eyes, he loses his power.

When we bring home the present moment and take responsibility for it with acceptance and attentiveness, it provides in the moment the energy we need to imagine the future with greater creativity. One technique for remembering to appreciate the present moment and everything that makes us happy is performing exercises in gratitude.

Exercising Gratitude

With mindfulness we train our ability to be in the present moment. Our thoughts often take us for a trip into the future, trying to get us ready for coming events or speculating about how things might happen. Or they take us to the past, where old memories and incidents can fill our thoughts and feelings and cause us to forget to be present here and now. In this exercise, we'll practice coming home to the present moment. One way to remember that the present is good in itself is to practice gratitude (Emmons and McCullough 2003; McCullough, Tsang and Emmons 2004). Through gratitude exercises, we'll train ourselves to value the here and now and everything that we're happy for in life.

Good Advice

Studies have shown that keeping a gratitude diary promotes happiness. If you feel you benefited from the exercise, you may want to start keeping a gratitude diary. Start the diary off by writing down three things you're grateful for. Do this three times a week over a period of five weeks. At first you'll find that remembering the things you're thankful for promotes even more thankfulness and satisfaction. In time, your gratitude will expand and fill you in moments when you're not writing in your gratitude diary.

Mindfulness Exercise
GRATITUDE

Take five minutes to practice mindfulness by observing your in-breath and out-breath.

1. Write down the three things you're grateful for in your work as a teacher:

_____

_____

_____

_____

_____

2. Write down why you're grateful for these things:

_____

_____

_____

_____

_____

3. What thoughts and feelings did this exercise evoke in you?

_____

_____

_____

_____

CHAPTER 6
How to Practice Mindfulness

ONE TIME WE GAVE A PRESENTATION to a couple hundred people at a university in Denmark. The theme of the presentation was Mindfulness in Education and it was attended by teachers from all the different disciplines. The event ran over four hours and we'd prepared a range of short introductions combined with mindfulness exercises, written reflections, dialogues with neighbors, and Q&A sessions.

As the event unfolded, we realized that some of the participants had clearly come expecting a four-hour long lecture covering, in minute detail, all of the concepts in our book. Each of the participants had bought the book along with their ticket, and now they sat with their books in front of them. The auditorium was fitted with projectors, microphones, chalkboards that could be raised or lowered, whiteboards, dusters, flipcharts, audio equipment, and loudspeakers. There we stood with just ourselves, and a few illustrations Didde drew on the chalkboard.

We believe that the science behind mindfulness is fascinating and important to understand. But when you get right down to it, mindfulness is a way of being present in the world. It's an experience-based practice; the only real way to learn about it is to practice it and make it a part of your life. After the event at the university, we stood there with chalk on our hands and it became very clear to us that we wanted not only to teach people about mindfulness, we wanted to share with them the experience of mindfulness.

If you wish to enjoy the benefits of mindfulness, it's necessary to set aside time for a mindfulness practice. In the beginning, set aside five, ten, or twenty minutes in the morning or evening to practice each day. It's important that you choose an amount of time that's practical for you so it can become a part of your daily life. It's better to begin with five minutes, rather than start with thirty minutes and then give up because you can't fit it into your life.

Be Aware of the Breath

Sit straight with your back upright and relaxed, in a place where you feel secure and comfortable. Set the clock and try to enjoy the time. Remind yourself that the intention of this practice is to foster joy and reduce suffering. Then pay attention to your breathing. Notice what takes place in and around you. Simply note it without making judgments or drawing conclusions about it. If you notice a disturbance, simply notice it. If you start to think, "I've got no time for this!" just try to accept that that's what you think. It's no problem unless you make it a problem. Try to go easy on yourself and continue to be at one with what you experience. Again and again, with an attitude of compassionate resolve, bring your attention back to your breathing, which is your anchor to the here and now. Each time you return to your breathing you exercise your "attention muscles." So there's no need to reproach yourself when your attention flutters away from the breath. Daily, persistent practice is important, as mindfulness is like exercising the muscles—it has to be done regularly to keep in training.

Let Causes Unveil Themselves

When we practice mindfulness meditation, we let our breathing be our friend. We're one with it, and we let it deepen. It takes time to be with our breathing. If it isn't deep, we take note of it without doing anything about it except to be one with it and it will naturally grow deeper. We don't need to put anything extra into our breathing; we simply let it be. In the first couple of breaths we can exhale a little more air than usual, but otherwise, we're simply at one with our breathing. If a thought arises like, "This isn't working, and I don't like it," we don't have to pretend that we don't feel that sense of irritation. We see the irritation and accept it. We don't need to worry about why we're irritated; we let the causes reveal themselves.

Accepting the Present Moment

Don't identify yourself with anything you notice in your attention during meditation. If you think, "I'm no good at this," you should try to see that without having to feel "I'm no good at anything." If you feel that you're getting nowhere, let it be. You aren't trying to change your feelings. Instead, you accept that's how you feel. Acceptance will take care of the feelings. It's all right to be full of impossible feelings and thoughts, but it's not all right to do nothing about it; and what we do is to be at one with the difficult feeling in a mood of acceptance. We accept the present moment.

Let Go

Let go, surrendering yourself to the present moment and the flow of life. We're in the present moment. Our awareness is broad and we make no judgments. Every moment we begin anew, over and over. When we try to control the moment, our actions become either habitual, so that we run on autopilot, or too controlling, so that we try to hold on to what is good. When we let go, we allow there to be space in the here and now and we meet others with generosity. We let go and surrender ourselves to the present moment. Each moment is fresh and new.

Let Everything Fall into Place

During meditation, thoughts and feelings gradually become quieter, and we experience clarity and joy in living. Before meditation, our state of mind can be unclear, like a freshly poured glass of homemade apple juice, in which the pulp makes the juice cloudy. Through meditation we let the pulp sink to the bottom of the glass by seeing and accepting it. Then we achieve a peaceful, transparent clarity. We can bring this peace and clarity to our interactions with other people. This apple-juice metaphor is found in the book *The Sun My Heart* by Thich Nhat Hanh.

Everyday Meditation

When we've established our basic mindfulness practice, we can more effectively bring mindfulness into the rest of our life. Informal meditation is everyday meditation. For instance, when you're writing on a computer, you can return every so often to being aware of your breathing and then continue to write. You may want to smile; it's joyful and relaxing. You can download from the Internet a meditation bell that can be made to ring at a certain time. The bell can be used as a periodic encouragement to remind you that once again, it's time to be aware. When the bell sounds, you can take a second to practice mindfulness. Gradually, the practice will become well established and contribute to your way of being in the world. For instance, while talking to someone, you can be conscious that you're talking with another person.

Slowly, your consciousness builds based on what takes place in the here and now, and that imparts actuality and richness to the situation.

One of the great advantages of mindfulness practice is that we strengthen our capacity to make the right decisions from the start. Being present in the moment and aware of our body, thoughts, and feelings often allows us to know the right thing to do in a given situation. But when we're harassed and unfocused, it's all too easy to make wrong decisions. Frequently wrong decisions need to be followed by the work of clearing up, unraveling the threads, and retracing our steps to the beginning. Unforeseen things surface quite often when working with a group of children, whether in a school or another setting. In such situations, the teacher's mindfulness practice is a tremendous support in maintaining calm, and in being able to see the whole picture, which forms the basis of good decision making.

The Mindfulness Traffic Lights

This tool serves to remind us of the three important steps in mindfulness practice. They can be hung in the classroom or somewhere easily seen, to remind us to practice mindfulness. (You may print out the mindfulness model from the back page of our free eWorkbook at www.stillnessrevolution.edu.)

The red light at the top lets traffic know that it's time to stop, in order to prevent accidents. It reminds us that it's time to change inappropriate habit patterns and to create happiness. The amber light in the middle shows that we admit acceptance and honesty into our thoughts, feelings, and senses. When we notice a feeling, we don't let resentment form around it; neither do we allow ourselves to fall prey to the feeling. Instead, we accept that the feeling of resentment is present. The green light, lowest of the lights, shows that we're clear and present, able to proceed and contribute and respond consciously to the situations that arise.

FIGURE 4:1. Mindfulness Traffic Lights show three important phases in mindfulness practice.

STOP   Stop and have the intention to create joy. Notice your breath with a mood of compassionate awareness. After a while, lay your hand on your upper abdomen so that you can be aware of your breathing.

ACCEPT   Notice what arises in your awareness with acceptance and without identifying yourself with the contents of your awareness. Smile.

CONTRIBUTE   Maintain contact with your breath and your presence in the here and now. Contribute in the best possible way with regard to the situation.

Challenges to Basic Mindfulness Practice

It's not always easy to maintain mindfulness practice. It requires persistence and a methodical approach to learning new habits. This can challenge us as we try to establish our own practice. So we recommend finding a teacher and supportive materials in order to get started. Otherwise it's all too easy to feel that we're alone in trying to maintain our practice and that we lack guidance.

Here are some of the challenges we may encounter when we try to set up a mindfulness practice.

- The feeling that we're short on time can cause us to stop mindfulness practice before we've properly started. We live in a culture in which time is in short supply. Mindfulness practice can soon become the thing we put aside in our busy daily routines when we don't believe it's as critical as all the other things we have to do. So it can be important to practice at a fixed time, using a clock or bell to time the meditation period.

- We get bored, fall asleep, become distracted, or experience irritation during meditation. The two common polarities of torpor and agitation can create disturbances as we practice. The art here is to become more insistent when we feel boredom, and let go more when we experience distractions. Mindfulness isn't just a relaxation technique. It's a practice in training our awareness and insight. Proper awareness can be compared with a stringed instrument: when the strings aren't too tight or too loose, the touch will be just right and the instrument will be in tune.

- When we sit in silence, many thoughts can arise, and we can become restless. These thoughts are always present, but now we become aware of them. Go ahead and become aware of them. Accept them and become good friends with them. They'll soon grow calm, and then, so can we.

- We believe we must empty our mind of all thoughts. The mind cannot and should not be emptied of thoughts. Thoughts grow peaceful when met with acceptance and relaxed breathing.

- We believe we must accept everything. When we practice mindfulness, we work a lot with acceptance of the thoughts, feelings, and sense impressions that fill us. We strive to accept others and ourselves as the people we are, but we don't have to accept our own or others' inappropriate behavior. We thereby make a distinction between the person and the behavior.

- Must we never be spontaneous or get angry anymore? Through mindfulness we learn to recognize, accept, and take our undesirable emotions in hand, including those that arise spontaneously. This lessens the risk that we spread negativity to ourselves and others.

- We feel we must work toward a definite goal or a definite way of being. Mindfulness takes as a starting point that we're already good enough, and the here and now is the place where awareness must dwell. Each time we hanker after something, we're no longer in the here and now, but tied to something in the future. It's one of the paradoxes of training in meditation that we wish to move on in our meditation practice. But the way from A to B is to be completely and utterly in A.

CHAPTER 7
Deep Breathing Creates Inner Calm

OUR BREATH IS THE ANCHOR FOR THE ENTIRE PRACTICE, the place we return to again and again when our thoughts lead our awareness astray, or into the future, or back into the past. With our breathing it's possible to calm the body, feelings, and thinking. The following tale shows how essential our breathing is.

The Source of Life

There was a meeting of all the human abilities, of which there are six, according to Indian tradition: the five senses plus thinking. As in so many meetings, first they had to decide who was going to make the decisions. Up jumped Sight and demonstrated his claim by creating beautiful pictures that delighted everyone. Smell came forth and created strong and unforgettable fragrances that left everyone with a feeling of excited expectation. But Taste went one step further than that with bewildering and vivid tastes from all the kitchens of the world. Hearing created wonderful harmonies that brought tears to everyone's eyes, and Touch called forth sensations that filled everyone with ecstasy. Thinking conjured up intellectual theories whose beautiful, deep truths impressed everyone.

Then came Breath, who was not numbered among the senses. All she could produce were simple inhalations and exhalations, which were not especially impressive compared with the other presentations. No one even noticed her. The other senses started a violent quarrel about who should be chosen to make decisions. Disappointed, Breath went away, and at once, the pictures began to fade, the tastes lost their savor, and sounds grew weaker. "Wait," cried the senses, "Come back! You shall decide for us. We need you." And Breath returned and took her rightful place (Rosenberg 2004).

An Overworked Heart

Didde: In 1995 when I was twenty, I traveled alone to Israel. I was very into poetry, and I had read a Danish poet's anthology titled *Territorial Song: A Jerusalem Composition.* The poet was inspired to write the anthology after her trip to Israel. I decided to follow in the footsteps of the poet and visit Israel. I planned a three-month trip and filled my backpack with things, including the anthology, which was my lodestar for the journey. It was early spring, and I planned to be in Jerusalem for Easter. After a longer trip around the northern part of the country, I found myself at the bus depot in Jerusalem at Eastertime. I wanted to go to Eilat, the country's southernmost town. As I wondered if there would be any other female passengers besides myself, the bus filled up with young Israeli soldiers.

After an hour, I realized we were heading south by another route than the one I expected. We were on our way into the Occupied Territories on the West Bank. After driving through that golden land-scape, we drove into the town of Hebron. Suddenly we heard gunshots and cries outside and all the soldiers bent over, their heads between their knees and the rifles on their backs pointed up into the sky. I followed their example and then heard a crashing noise against the bus and more shouting. I had no idea what was happening. Was this the end? The journey through the Holy Land had taken a dramatic turn, as reality cut through my romantic notions and my naiveté. Furious at the presence of a busful of Israeli soldiers, the Palestinian population hurled rocks at the bus. After some intense minutes during which I had no idea whether I would live or die, the bus started off again.

The bus resumed its way to Eilat and dropped the soldiers off at Israeli defense posts on the way through the West Bank. They were going back to work after celebrating Passover in Jerusalem. After some days in Eilat, I noticed I wasn't feeling too well. Although I still had a month left to go on my trip, I went to Tel Aviv, changed my ticket, and flew home.

Three weeks after coming home, I became seriously ill. All the fine balances of my body had fallen out of sync. I was constantly tired, my hands shook, and my nervous system was on overdrive. I skipped periods, my heart hammered violently in my chest, and my breathing was disturbed. The inner peace I'd previously been known for was gone. My violent heartbeat reminded me that at least I was still alive. My body and my psyche had received a shock.

It took me many years to recover my balance in body and mind and find inner peace. I started with allopathic medicines and made many other changes in my lifestyle. Then, meditation came into the picture, and subsequently, I discovered mindfulness.

Coherence

Our breath has a powerful influence on our state of being—mental, physical, and emotional. The extreme polarities of breathing are a deep, harmonious breath at one pole and chaotic breathing at the other. The condition of our breath affects our body, feelings, and thinking in different ways. Disorderly breathing is stressful and harmonious breathing creates inner calm. When we're stressed, anxious, depressed, or angry, it affects the variability of the rhythm of our heart. When we experience conditions of well-being, sympathy, and gratitude, the variability becomes "coherent," which means that the shift between rising and falling heart rhythms is regular. Maintaining a state of heart coherence, with its positive effects on the natural variability of our blood pressure and other functions, can help prevent stress. See Appendix 2 on page 127 for more on coherence.

Deep Breathing

How do we train ourselves in coherence and what are the consequences? A school administrator who suffered from stress had his heart rhythm measured throughout his working day. The results showed that the administrator's heart, particularly in meetings with the principal—who often put people down, and was habitually cynical—was in an unhealthy and chaotic state (Servan-Schreiber 2004). The administrator learned in the course of two months' training to concentrate on the sensations in his chest to maintain his composure and coherence. The coherence method is based on deep breathing, the basis of mindfulness practice. Slow, deep breaths stimulate the parasympathetic nervous system and help slow down the pulse.

To achieve coherence, our awareness should follow each deep breath in and out to the end of the exhalation, and then pause for a couple of seconds before the next breath begins. Coherence fosters coordination among the brain's activities, which leads to quicker, more precise reactions and an enhanced capacity to perform under pressure. Coherence cultivates a greater ability to make judgments and increases decision-making competence. Simultaneously, the amount of coherence lowers the stress hormone cortisol and increases the immune system's immunoglobulin A, which is the body's first line of defense against harmful microorganisms that can cause illness, whether viral, bacterial, or fungal.

Mindfulness practice trains coherence as long as we continue to allow our breathing to be relaxed and deep. When we train ourselves in mindfulness, we observe our breathing. Breathing is the anchor in our mindfulness practice; the place we revisit again and again when thoughts drive our awareness into the future or back into the past. Through the breathing we can bring calm to our bodies, feelings, and thoughts.

The purposes of training awareness of the breath are:

- To let our breathing grow deeper and more harmonious, thereby strengthening our inner calm
- To give a basic technique for peace that you can use in your teaching; for example, if there's a lot of unrest during a lesson or in a group
- To make others calm through your calm
- To see clearly what's happening around you

Good Advice

When you work with awareness of the breath, sooner or later you'll experience that your awareness either flutters away into thoughts, becomes full of feelings, or notices a physical pain in the body. When you realize that your awareness has wandered away from observing your breathing, move it back to breathing in and breathing out. This is the basic exercise.

It's a good idea to choose a fixed time in the day for the exercise, and set your alarm clock so you don't need to think about the time.

If you get a pain in your back, leg, or another place in your body while you're observing your breathing, adjust your position a little. You might need support for your back or an extra cushion to sit on so your pelvis can be lifted a little higher. It's important to find a comfortable position so you can be peaceful.

Be careful not to hyperventilate; just let your breathing come and go. It's important that you're able to notice your breathing slowly becoming deeper; as you do, you'll feel more rested.

Awareness of the breath is the central practice in mindfulness. You'll find that good contact with your breath is also an important tool that you can use in your teaching work to find calm in all the situations that arise over the course of the day.

Mindfulness Exercise
BREATH AWARENESS

Sit comfortably on a chair or cushion, perhaps with your eyes closed. Your back should be straight and relaxed. Turn your awareness to your in-breath and out-breath. Follow your in-breath and out-breath with your awareness, and try not to alter your breathing. Don't try to make it deeper. Just observe the breath as it is. Use the next five minutes to observe your breathing.

CHAPTER 8

Stress Reduction through Mindfulness

CASE STUDY: Back to School!
Søren Bogø, Grade-School Teacher, Denmark

In the spring, I took an unwanted break from my job as a teacher. After many sleepless nights and failed attempts at coping with the high demands of my job during the day, I was forced to take time off due to stress.

Two months later I was back. I had been successful at reducing my stress levels and my lurking depression had given way to a new faith in my work as a teacher. Still, I had to find my footing again back at school. My school administrator suggested I attend a mindfulness course during the new school year. It became a weekly occurrence, and when the eight weeks were up, I liked it so much I decided to repeat it again.

The mindfulness course taught me how important it is to remain open to sense impressions, how important it is not to rush to judgments, and how important it is to let others break through my defenses. All this came about because I was reminded to breathe. What an awakening! The effects spread like ripples in a pond. Dreary meetings became meaningful. Passing experiences began to integrate themselves harmoniously. I felt a warmth coming from the world—from all over, not just from colleagues and students. Could mindfulness do all that?

Mindfulness is not an antistress vaccine, but it gives us greater calm in meeting our many impressions and challenges. We're able to keep several balls in the air, even those that fall! As teachers, we're very much "on" in teaching, and if the challenges grow too numerous or too great, the endless round of self-incrimination begins. We judge ourselves for being helplessly behind, and there's no immediate relief on the way. We become our own worst critic, and self-reproach is our ever-increasing punishment.

Mindfulness with children begins with ourselves. If the teacher's life leaves us feeling ragged and washed out, we can't really meet the children. Mindfulness is anchored firmly in the breath, and it loosens energy that would otherwise be trapped. It ought to be an integral part of teaching. Mindfulness isn't about losing ourselves in distant goals, but about being present in the here and now. Children are good "mid-wives" in this regard, and it's wonderful to be part of the present again.

One of the potential stress-producing factors in the job of teaching is the need for control. I was a control freak, happily directing the teaching in a certain way. Being in control isn't in itself a negative thing, but it takes a lot of energy. This energy can become rigid and teaching become one-way communication—"tank-filling education," if you will, with the students as the tank and the teacher as the attendant at the gas pump.

When I came back after my sick leave, I felt far more confidence in myself and in the children; a theme touched on in the Hans Christian Andersen story, "The Bell," which we were working on in the sixth grade. The story is about not stopping or turning back the first time you believe you've found what you're looking for (the chime of the bell). Another story we read was "Something" (Andersen again), which is about how we achieve something in life. It's one of Andersen's most thought-provoking stories, and it became the basis for a collection of dazzling poems the students wrote under the heading "Something." There was an empathy in our experiences together, which we all felt.

Now the children are on their way to the high school in town, and I'm continuing my life as a teacher. Hans Christian Andersen helped us on our way, but so did the mood in the classroom, perhaps because I wasn't so dreadfully anxious about losing control. Control is good, but trust is better.

Søren Bogø participated in one of Nikolaj's mindfulness courses, as did Dorte Møller and Martin Ammentorp, who describe their experiences later in the book.

Stress

The sad reality is that many who work in the field of education are laid low by stress at one time or another. Stress is a problem in many ways. Many experience tiredness and depression; they lose their composure; it affects their memory and outlook; and their interpersonal skills decline rapidly. Stressed coworkers are often ineffective and fragile.

Stress affects the realm of the brain called the frontal lobes and it significantly impairs mental abilities. Research has shown that the frontal lobes are the area where a person develops goals, makes plans for achieving them, and evaluates afterward whether her actions have led to success or failure (Goldberg 2002). The frontal lobes are also the place where a person registers what she needs, and where her own mental state is registered. The frontal lobes are also the decisive factor when we encounter choices, where there is not only one option, but a multiplicity of possible options. The frontal lobes are the primary coordinators and direct the other parts of the brain. It's through the frontal lobes that we distinguish another's state of being, which is the basis for empathy.

The amygdala is the almond-shaped nucleus in the part of our brain connected with feelings, and it has the function of alerting us to danger. The frontal lobes take care to check whether there's anything

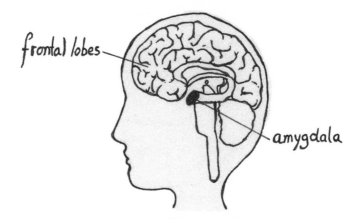

FIGURE 6:2. The position of the frontal lobes and the amygdala in the brain.

to be worried about. For instance, you might be in a dark room and see something that looks like a snake. This activates the amygdala. When you turn the light on, you see the "snake" is actually a piece of rope, which means you no longer have to be on your guard. The frontal lobes direct the amygdala, but they lose that function when we're stressed.

Stress overloads the frontal lobes, which explains why decisions made under stress can be poor ones. The stress sufferer has difficulty in knowing what he needs, and is often unaware of his mental state. Similarly, he has difficulty developing goals and strategies for taking action, evaluating actions, or making decisions when a number of options present themselves. All this is because his frontal lobes are overburdened. The frontal lobes are flooded with a high cortisol level and an amygdala that can't be controlled anymore.

> A rider came galloping full tilt past another man, who called out: "Where are you off to in such a hurry?" The rider replied: "Ask the horse!" (Nhat Hanh 1999).

Mindfulness Strengthens the Frontal Lobes

Research shows that mindfulness generally strengthens the frontal lobes, which, among other things, leads to an increased ability to empathize with others and to make complex decisions. We know that many teachers experience tremendous pressure in their daily work. Seen in this light, mindfulness is a necessary preventative measure against stress in the educational setting. By practicing mindfulness we can prevent stress and become better at understanding our students, create a better learning environment, and increase their healthy development (Siegel 2007).

The restoration function is an important skill in stress management. This refers to the length of time it takes us to return to a normal, peaceful state after we've been in the grip of a difficult emotion. Mindfulness strengthens the restoration function (Goleman 2004). In one experiment, upsetting and threatening images were shown to volunteers. Some of the volunteers showed stronger activity in their left frontal lobes, which indicates that these individuals were better at holding amygdala activity in check, and so better able to achieve happiness. The research shows that people with brain activity in the left frontal lobe are able to express feelings of good fortune, happiness, enthusiasm, and high energy. Those individuals who recovered more quickly after viewing the images also had a lower level of cortisol, the stress hormone. People who recover more quickly from upsetting experiences also have better immune reactions. These individuals are found to have a higher degree of cell breakdown activity, which indicates that their immune systems are better able to fight off sickness (Davidson 2003).

In many schools, we find a high degree of illness among teachers. It diminishes students' learning outcomes when their teachers are sick, and it's a drain on the school's resources. From an economic point of view, mindfulness practice can be a very cost-effective way to reduce time off for sickness.

Being the Students' Frontal Lobes

Nikolaj: When we returned from our visit to Plum Village, I was working at a twenty-four-hour therapeutic center for families, which had a little classroom connected to it. Most of the families were single moms and their kids, and they had so many social and emotional problems that there was a risk the children would be removed from their families. It was my job to teach these exposed and sometimes highly explosive children. But how could I teach children who were in danger of being taken from their mothers, children in emotional chaos, children whose amygdalas were brimming over? Since I had just come back from a mindfulness retreat, I wondered if maybe I could use what I had learned there to create more peace in these children.

One day, I sat behind two seven-year-olds who were trying to work on projects in their workbooks. But they couldn't concentrate. They needed *my* frontal lobes to keep their attention directed to their projects. Without inner calm and concentration, there can be no learning. So I sat right behind the two childen and "became their frontal lobes," supporting them with care and concentration again and again. Each time their attention wandered away from their work, I calmed them down with my own calm and directed their attention back to the work. Slowly they became more peaceful and concentrated.

Many of these children had been damaged early in life and had endured the long-term effects of stress. It was impossible to expect them to instantaneously concentrate for long periods of time. But just as the brain can be altered by the effects of chronic stress, it's also true that, with mindfulness, we can bring about positive changes.

Neuroplasticity: How Mindfulness Alters the Brain

The manner in which we focus our awareness changes the brain. This means that we have the possibility of affecting our brain's development, and this can be registered in the brain structure. When we focus our awareness on developing a skill and continue to do so over time, the skill that is practiced gradually becomes a character trait. Our neurons fire whenever we have an experience. Neural firing strengthens existing neurons and stimulates the growth of new neurons, which creates new synaptic connections (a synapse is a point of contact between two brain cells).

Neuroplasticity is the term used when the synaptic connection changes as a reaction to an experience. "Neurons that fire together wire together," as brain scientists say. This means neurons that fire simultaneously will connect. Put simply, we can see the changes in the brain when a new skill is learned: new pathways form in the brain.

The Monk Spreads Calm and Happiness

MRI scans that chart changes in brain activity have made it possible to study what happens in the brain during mindfulness meditation. A test done with a Western monk showed that he had significantly higher activity in his left frontal lobe than the other 174 people who participated in the study. The test shows that people with this brain activity manifest feelings of happiness, enthusiasm, and high energy. Heightened activity in the left frontal lobe was also present when the monk was not meditating. In another test, researchers played a recording of gunfire through the earphones the monk was wearing while he meditated. When they measured his stress level, it proved to be markedly lower than that of all the others who had undergone the same test.

As a social experiment, the monk's stress level was tested during conversations he had with a friendly professor and with a hostile professor. They discussed topics that they had little agreement on, such as reincarnation and why one should become a monk rather than a scientist. During the monk's discussion with the friendly professor, the video recording showed that they frequently smiled at each other. Afterward they spoke positively about the discussion, and both wished to continue the exchange when the experiment was finished.

During the monk's conversation with the hostile professor, the latter began aggressively, but when the monk stayed calm, the professor himself grew more peaceful as the conversation continued. Later the professor said, "I wasn't able to be confrontational. I was met at all times with common sense and a smile; it was overwhelming. I could feel something—a bit like a shadow or a beam of light—and I was unable to be aggressive" (Goleman 2003). The monk's stress level was constant in both conversations. He smiled more, however, in conversation with the friendly professor. The hostile professor's stress level was high at first, and gradually grew lower and lower. The study concluded that a stressed-out or angry person can be calmed by speaking with a person who does not return their aggression, and who responds with calm and friendliness.

These different test results show how changes in people's brains gradually come about through daily mindfulness meditation. It also shows that we're able to create new habits that are meaningful for the way we live in the world. The monk's proficiency in relationships is extremely well developed; he holds his amygdala in check when exposed to pressure and does not react adversely. We know that a student's learning outcome depends to a high degree on the teacher's competence in educational relationships. If we, as teachers, develop the qualities the monk has developed through mindfulness, we shall strengthen our competence in relations and in affecting our students' learning outcomes.

CHAPTER 9

How Mindfulness Strengthens Our Relationships

WHEN WE OBSERVE ANOTHER PERSON displaying a particular emotion, it activates nerve cells in our brain—called mirror neurons—that can direct us to experience that same emotion. This is known as neurobiological resonance, and it happens spontaneously, without our having to think about it. Mirror resonance gives us the opportunity to notice what other people are feeling. These signals form an important basis for decisions we may make. Mirror resonance also explains how stress, zest for life, and other feelings and moods can be contagious.

Feelings are particularly contagious when they come from authority figures. In schools and kindergartens, children are often subjected to the effects of their teachers' emotional states. This means in everyday educational situations the teacher must always be aware of evoking mirror reactions in a child through her behavior, her mood, eye contact, and body language.

Nikolaj: In my work with school development, I met a remarkable principal. I remember him vividly, partly because he was so flexible in his ideas, and partly because of his gift for creating a friendly, pleasant environment at his school. Each morning, rain or shine, the principal stood in the schoolyard and wished parents and students good morning. He knew the names of all the students and their parents, and he was vigilant about whether there was anything he should know about them that had a bearing on the learning situation. He was at their disposal in a friendly and obliging way and could take things as they came

The principal's office was a power source where anyone could visit and be reenergized. He always had the abundance to deal with issues both great or small, and all who met him went on their way with renewed vigor. The spirit he brought to his work created a good atmosphere in the whole school that affected everyone who came into contact with the place.

Conversely, I've been in schools where the principal spreads a heavy and torpid mood. This puts a damper on the teachers' possibilities and commitment as well as on the learning environment they create, and it affects the students' learning outcomes.

Feelings are contagious

Our understanding of mirror neurons makes it clear that people influence each other much more than we'd think. Mirror-neuron resonance causes us to infect other people contagiously with positive as well as negative feelings. Julia's bad mood can become Joseph's bad mood. Rosa's feelings of joy can become Laura's feelings of joy. This neurobiological-resonance activity can also help us develop empathy, as we gradually practice our ability to observe what is happening in other people. As we develop and refine this capacity, it can become intuition. Through mirror resonance, we can have a spontaneous, intuitive understanding of what motivates another person, when we can perceive in ourselves the underlying purpose of her actions and feelings.

We've often observed that students who are seen in a bad light by the teacher find themselves caught in a negative cycle. The teacher becomes more and more frustrated, and that reduces her empathy considerably. And when empathy for the student is reduced, the student behaves more and more badly. The fundamental confidence is broken, and the teacher has difficulty seeing the situation clearly.

When we're in an agitated state, we can't take in information that doesn't maintain or justify the feelings that consume us. This creates misperceptions in the way we see ourselves and the world (Ekman 2003). For instance, if we become upset with some of our students' parents, we may focus on their personal character traits and behavior, and that underpins our antipathy towards them. We see them in a negative light, and are blind to their good sides.

In one study, two people were placed opposite each other with instructions not to talk or communicate through facial expressions or gestures. After several minutes in silence, they came to share the same feelings. Researchers discovered that transmission of feelings depends on which of the subjects feels more strongly, or which has the higher status (Petty et al 2003; Friedman 1981).

Strongest Feelings Win

Feelings are social, and in gatherings of people, they can have consequences. This phenomenon also extends to biology. Heart rhythm, blood pressure, body temperature, immune system, oxygen uptake, sugar levels, and hormones can also be "spread" and changed (Lewis et al. 2000). Research has shown that the staff on cardiac wards can affect the state of heart patients in a positive way through palliative treatment. The palliative worker's own state of being lowers the patient's blood pressure and limits the release of the fatty acids that block the arteries (Berkman 1992). Studies have also measured a spike in the blood pressure of people who work for a boss who frequently expresses negative emotions (Wagner et al. 2003). Other research shows that after two hours spent working together, the members of a working group tend to share the same mental attitude (Bartel 2000).

These findings cast new light on the culture of meetings in the field of education, in which the person with the strongest feelings or greatest power tends to affect the rest of the group. Many teachers have sat through meetings from which people emerged tired, cranky, and in a bad mood. When we think back over a meeting, we can take note of which feelings came from whom, and whether we let ourselves be carried away or tried to spread our own positivity and joy. The free expression of an emotion, regardless of whether it's negative or positive, tends to intensify that emotion in us as individuals and as a group.

Our behavior doesn't simply affect others; we can also "catch" the contagion by grumbling, nagging, or smiling. In research, we differentiate between a genuine smile and a superficial smile. The genuine smile is called a Duchenne smile, after the French neurologist Guillaume Duchenne. It engages the muscles around the eyes and the mouth, which only happens when we genuinely feel happy. Mindfulness can intensify happiness through gratitude, friendliness, and genuine smiling. If, on the other hand, we wish to shut down our negative emotional resonance, we can avert our attention so it isn't contagious. If we find that we "spread contagion" by thinking of a given situation, we can maintain calm by trying to detach ourselves and reconciling ourselves to the situation. It's more difficult for children to close off their emotional resonance because their frontal lobes are less developed. This increases the teacher's responsibility not to transmit negative emotions to the children in her care.

Marked Mirroring

Marked mirroring is a tool that can be used in meetings with children, parents, or colleagues who may approach us full of negativity. When we "mark," we show a mirroring activity that is harmonious with the other's state of being, yet not identical to it. We simply mark or note it, without taking the other person's negative or sad emotional state upon ourselves. Marked mirroring is a tool that can be used to show empathy, avoid negative contagion, and increase positivity.

For example, we hear the sound of crying in the kindergarten, and we hurry to see what has happened. We find that Alicia has fallen and cut her knee. We can respond to Alicia in different ways. Clearly, if we tell Alicia she is being silly and she should stop crying, she will not feel cared for. On the other hand, if we show a high degree of involvement with Alicia's drama, she will cry even more loudly, because she believes something really serious has happened to her and the ambulance is on its way with sirens blaring. In that case we have exaggerated the mirroring, which causes Alicia's feelings of pain and discomfort to grow.

The quality of our tone of voice is of great significance when a child hurts herself or is upset in some other way. The same applies to the quality of our contact. The way we talk to or touch a child is far more significant than what we say to her. We tend to think our words are the most comforting thing we can offer, but actually the care we put into our contact is far stronger. So it's a good idea to avoid using too many words. Instead, expose Alicia to calm feelings by having her "catch" them from our peaceful tone of voice and gentle touch.

While smiling is contagious and increases positivity, sometimes there are situations where a smile isn't productive. Reuben is upset because he's been teased during recess. He needs, first of all, to feel met in his mood. By meeting Reuben where he's at, we can gradually turn the situation around. Marked mirroring presupposes that we can tune in to Reuben's "frequency." That requires a heightened awareness that helps us perceive Reuben's inner state. That's the starting point from which we estimate how to meet Reuben on the subtle basis that constitutes marked mirroring. Mindfulness practice can support the development of heightened awareness.

Defense Mechanisms

As teachers, we can have difficulty accepting the fact that we play a part in our students' poor development or lack of learning. We have observed many times that a parent who contacts her child's teacher because the child isn't thriving at school is rebuffed or met with blame. When the teacher either denies that there are problems with the child's growth or lays the responsibility on the parent, it's difficult for them to work constructively together. The teacher's defense mechanisms block his willingness to have an open mind about the situation and take his share of the responsibility in solving the problem.

We're all guided by psychic defense mechanisms that we use to reduce or banish experiences of strong, unpleasant feelings. Examples of psychic defense mechanisms include denial, projection, intellectualizing, idealizing, and splitting.

In situations where we allow ourselves to be attacked by another's negativity, *denial* is an obvious psychic mechanism to use in self-defense. With denial we shut our eyes to the situation and pretend that the attack hasn't found its target.

We can also use *idealizing*, in which we see only the good in every situation, repress the bad, and pretend that everything is fine.

Projection implies that we transfer an inner conflict on to someone else; a mechanism we often use if we're stressed. We get rid of the difficult feelings by projecting them out into the environment. For instance, we might blame the parents of a girl we find difficult to control in class for not having brought up their daughter properly, even though that's only one part of the story.

The defense mechanism of *splitting* means that we can't handle ambivalence, and so we divide the world into black and white. Through splitting, we try to gain control over a situation we experience with growing anxiety.

Our psychic defense mechanisms are hard at work distancing us from those things that are hard to look in the eye, from breakdowns in relationships to experiences that create feelings of inadequacy. Through mindfulness it becomes possible to create other methods of coping with difficult situations so that we avoid dependence on defense mechanisms. In that way we can change our inappropriate habits. As the following story shows, we have to work to get rid of our inappropriate defense mechanisms.

The Princess and the Dragon

Once upon a time, a king and queen found themselves in debt to a dragon. To relieve themselves of this debt, they entered into a bargain to marry their daughter, the princess, to the dragon. The princess was very unhappy about this bargain and went to a wise woman to seek advice. The wise woman told her she should not complain, but simply follow her instructions. When the wedding day dawned, the princess followed the old woman's advice and put on ten thin dresses. On the wedding night, the princess asked the dragon if he'd remove his clothes at the same time she did, so she wouldn't be too embarrassed. The dragon agreed to the bargain. Each time the princess took off a layer of clothing, the dragon had to take off a layer. First the princess took off her wedding dress, and the dragon took off his fine suit. He was surprised to see that she had on another dress underneath, which she removed. The dragon, who had no more clothes on, had to take off his scales, instead. This was not hard for the dragon, for he often shed his scales. Next the princess took off her third dress and the dragon had to dig a little deeper to

79

remove his next layer of skin. The princess took off her fourth dress, and the dragon now had to use his claws to scrape off his next layer. It was painful, but he wanted to keep to the bargain he'd made with the princess. And so it went, and when they'd removed their eighth layer, the princess saw that the dragon had changed his form. When the dragon had taken off his last layer, he stood before her as a handsome young prince. (Freely retold from the adventures of King Lindorm.)

Just like the dragon in the fairy tale, we can work on abandoning our defense mechanisms and negative habits, with the help of mindfulness practice. The teacher who used to protect himself through denial or blame can learn to have the courage to look at complex situations with an open mind and conduct himself honestly and candidly.

Exposure

For us, exposure is a very powerful and central aspect of mindfulness. Exposure means that we allow the sense impressions, feelings and thoughts that permeate us to be there without suppressing them, thereby unveiling them. We are at peace with our sensations, thoughts and feelings, even though they can be difficult and burdensome.

Didde: I was very shy of conflict when I was young, and a bit too anxious to please. In discussions I would most often back down and let the other person be right. It was hard for me to be in tense situations with other people. The illusion that everything should be good all the time often wore me out, and sometimes caused me to be sick, as it was a hard premise to live by. Working with mindfulness and letting what is within oneself be there, no matter what it may be, has taught me that I don't have to avoid difficult feelings or thoughts.

Mindfulness Exercise
DEEP LISTENING

Zen Master Thich Nhat Hanh suggests this practice for learning how to listen deeply. The deep listening practice is to set the specific intention to listen without interruption. He says, "You have to practice breathing mindfully in and out so that compassion always stays with you. You listen without giving advice or passing judgment. You can say to yourself about the other person, I am listening to him just because I want to relieve his suffering. This is also called compassionate listening. You can listen in such a way that compassion remains alive in you the whole time you are listening. That is the art."

If halfway through listening, irritation or anger comes up, then take a break if you can. Every time that irritation and anger comes up, practice breathing in and out mindfully. No matter what the other person says, even if there is a lot of strong information and injustice in his way of seeing things, even if he condemns or blames you, continue to sit very quietly breathing in and out.

If you don't feel that you can continue to listen in this way, let the other person know that you need to take a break and will talk more another time soon. If you're not in good shape, you're not going to listen in the best way you can. Part of the practice of deep listening is being aware when you can do it and when you can't. The more you practice mindfulness techniques yourself, the more you'll be available to practice deep listening with colleagues, parents, and children.

Recently we were teaching mindfulness in a kindergarten. The teacher who had booked us had been working with the mindfulness exercises in our eWorkbook. During the workshop she was deeply touched emotionally, and when I spoke with her afterwards, the tears ran down her cheeks. She was right in the midst of the exposure process, where we let our defence mechanisms fall away and be with what is. At first it can bring about vulnerability. But gradually we learn to be in the world in this new way, and vulnerability is transformed into strength and authenticity.

CHAPTER 10
Mindfulness and Anger Management

FEELINGS CAN BE VIEWED AS MESSENGERS. Feelings of anger inform us that our values or expectations aren't being met, or that we haven't taken ourselves properly in hand. These difficult feelings can stand in the way of good relationships and a good learning environment. As teachers we're often pushed into confrontations with anger, whether we encounter it in ourselves, our students, or among colleagues.

Everyone has the seeds of anger in them. Whether or not the seeds sprout and grow into angry outbursts depends on how anger arises and whether it is nurtured. The vast majority of people cannot avoid showing anger once in a while. But will that anger spread and create a negative environment in which to work and learn? That depends on whether we try to manage anger or not.

We've all heard the myth that we should express our anger in order to get rid of it; after we've let off steam, we won't feel so tense and hot under the collar. But the causes for anger aren't gotten rid of. On the contrary, we may have expressed our anger in a way that's created more problems for others and ourselves. Anger breeds anger, and angry outbursts increase the stress level and prolong the anger. As discussed earlier, when the amygdala is out of control, it leads to stress. And when the amygdala runs wild, it also leads to aggression. A highly active amygdala lowers our ability to self-regulate (Davidson et al. 2000). We don't get rid of anger by expressing it (Zillmann 1993).

Research also shows that people who frequently have angry outbursts have an increased risk of blood clots (Barefoot 1985). In other words, anger is damaging to our health. Systematically expressing anger and negativity creates habits that easily lead to affective or instinctual reactions the next time we're emotionally challenged. This means that our threshold gets lower and lower, and we get angry more easily.

The Volcano Of Anger

The volcano of anger gives us a vivid image of the progress of anger, which, if not taken in hand, can explode in a volcanic eruption. Anger typically begins with unfulfilled expectations, disappointment—a feeling that things didn't turn out the way we wanted them to. Disappointment leads to irritation that our expectations weren't met. This is followed by accusations and blame. If we haven't already begun to feel physically strained, we certainly do now. Our pulse rate rises and our breath comes more quickly.

If we allow anger to escalate, we begin to think someone should be held responsible for this wretched business. We may begin to issue little threats, in which we think or say, "If this or that isn't properly cleared up, someone's going to get in trouble." These threats can be mixed with avoidance, in which we tell ourselves that we couldn't care less. By this stage, our blood pressure has risen, our muscles are tense, and we're filled with pain and anger and ready for battle. If we let the anger escalate further, it concludes with a big eruption that can be followed by overwhelming fatigue.

Figure 8:1. gives an overview of the phases of anger, so we can be on the lookout for the different steps in the escalation process. The illustration shows how the feelings arise. The earlier we're able to begin mindfulness practice, the sooner we can halt the escalation and take our anger in hand.

rage

anger

blame

irritation

unfulfilled expectations

FIGURE 8:1. The volcano of anger shows how we work ourselves up from irritation to anger and rage.

When Anger Arises

Ms. Trill teaches fourth-grade music. She always finishes her music lesson with one minute's silence before recess. Out in the corridor a boy from the fifth grade passes by, banging hard on the door of the music room. This is the third time in a row the boy has done this, and Ms. Trill can't hold her feelings in check any longer. She goes to the door, wrenches it open, and dashes after the boy, who is already half-way down the corridor. She grabs his arm, pulls him aside, and vents her anger on him. The episode ends with the trembling boy scurrying away down the hallway, while Ms. Trill returns to the music department. Red-faced, shaky all over, and heart pounding, she quickly finishes the lesson with the fourth grade. The rest of the day Ms. Trill is tired, fed up, and still angry, which her colleagues notice through her contagious feelings.

Mindfulness Practice Takes Anger in Hand

How can we deal with this kind of familiar situation in which anger runs away with a person? Through mindfulness practice we can work against the delusion of cathartic outbursts; that is, the misunderstanding that by venting our anger we can get rid of it. Ms. Trill was no less angry after scolding the boy—quite the reverse. Now her anger is refueled with exhaustion and irritation, and she's left with an unresolved situation. Instead of Ms. Trill expressing the anger that consumed her, it would help her to recognize the anger in herself, and breathe deeply, taking notice of it. Slowly she'd be able to notice that her breathing has a calming effect, and that she cools down. Next, Ms. Trill should work on accepting the anger; not to prolong or express it, but just to accept that it's there. This requires full awareness, and therefore experience with mindfulness practice is a great help.

It can be equally helpful to remember that we have the ability to step out of the mental drama, and instead bear witness to what fills our awareness in a nonjudgmental manner. In other words, we don't identify ourselves with our emotional state, because we know that feelings and thoughts are "guests" in our awareness. When Ms. Trill has taken control of her anger in this way, it dissolves, and now it's possible for her to create good management strategies consciously and constructively. She can go back to the boy who provoked her anger and resolve the disagreement once and for all. Obviously, it will also be necessary for her to speak with the boy's class teacher about a solution to the basic problem.

The Homecoming Soldier

Even the United States Army is using mindfulness training based on the stress reduction programs of Jon Kabat-Zinn, which have had great success in hospitals. One young army officer who had a hot temper and a history of anger- and stress-related problems was ordered by his superior to attend an eight-week mindfulness-training class to help reduce his stress level. One day, after attending the class for some weeks, he stopped for groceries on his way home. He was in a hurry and a bit

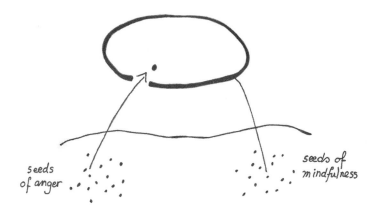

seeds of anger

seeds of mindfulness

FIGURE 8:2. The seeds of all feelings are found in everyone. If the seeds come into consciousness, they can be expressed. The seed of mindfulness can embrace and calm the seed of anger. (Illustration adapted from Nhat Hanh 1999).

irritated as usual. When he took his cart to check out, there were long lines. The woman in front of him, who had a baby with her, had only one item, but she wasn't in the express line. She was in the wrong line, talking and holding everyone up. Then she passed the baby to the cashier and the cashier spent a moment cooing over the child. The officer could feel his habitual anger rising. But because he'd been practicing mindfulness, he started to become aware of the heat and tightness in his body. He could feel the pain. He breathed and relaxed. When he looked up again, he saw the little boy smiling. As he reached the cashier, he said, "That was a cute boy."

"Oh, thank you!" she responded. "That's my baby. His father was in the Air Force, but he was killed last winter. Now I have to work full-time. My mom tries to bring my boy in once or twice a day so I can see him." (Kornfield 2008)

The next exercise is an example of the inner work the soldier did while he stood in the checkout line and felt himself becoming worked up and angry.

Mindfulness Exercise
ANGER

RECOGNIZE: When we become aware that we're angry, we stop and concentrate on our breathing. Perhaps we feel strained, our heart is beating faster, and perhaps we're taking shallow breaths. Breathing brings body and mind together and is calming. We observe our breathing without changing it.

ACCEPT: We accept that there's anger in us, without expressing it or repressing it. We try to hold the anger in an embrace like a mother holding her crying baby. The moment we try to accept pain is the moment when we can step into the conflagration. The equipment we need as a "firefighter" is compassion. Compassion can awaken and be kept alive through awareness of our breath. This step will give us peace and concentration, and clear the way for us to be able to see the deeper basis of the anger.

INSIGHT: Once calm and concentration are in place, we try to find the deeper reason for our pain and feelings of anger. Compassion leads us to understand why the pain is there. We have insight into our anger and can act out of that insight. (Adapted from Nhat Hanh 2002)

CHAPTER 11

Children and Mindfulness

MANY CHILDREN GROW UP IN BUSY FAMILIES, with their days packed full of activities. Families fill up their calendars, and many experience the growing problem of never having enough time. Aside from having to navigate their way through their own daily routines, children experience stressed-out adults who hurry from one place to the next. This hectic pace has consequences for children. Some grow up lacking positive contact with adults. Many parents have full-time jobs and a slew of other priorities that come before their children. When the pace of life is rapid, there's an increased need to digest the many impressions and choices everyday life offers. Families neglect to set aside time simply to be.

Children have grown used to a very high degree of entertainment, and relaxation often takes place in front of the TV or the computer. Here, new information presses in, and there seldom arises a silent space, in which everything that fills us up can have a chance to deposit itself and, in time, become primary experience. A hectic pace of life, multitasking, and sense bombardment can fragment awareness so we become restless.

Our homes have become vibrating platforms with the virtual door always open. We have our computer screens switched on, with games, emails, and Facebook updates constantly giving us information. World events roll into our living rooms from early in the morning until late at night on our TV screens. Our cell phones send us texts demanding to be answered here and now. Children rarely have the opportunity to play and relax in the home without being exposed to an electronic stream of information and entertainment. Computers and TV can certainly be educational at times, but they don't encourage children to be physically active or to sense their own needs and feelings. Kids become engrossed in the video game they're playing or the movie they're watching. They don't get around to sorting out the multitude of information that's presented to them, and that means such information can accumulate, causing mental, physical, or emotional stress.

Children and Mindfulness

Children who learn mindfulness through their upbringing have a great advantage. We live in an extrovert culture, and most children don't learn to orient themselves inwardly and become anchored in listening to their inner lives. There's an imbalance between the outer stimuli from the massive stream of information pouring in and their inner impulses—feelings, intuition, and deeper motivations.

Experience shows that children implanted with seeds of mindfulness gain the tools that will help them in many areas of their lives. For instance, a child can concentrate better, feel more settled, and have a greater capacity to notice his body, feelings, and thoughts (Greenland 2010). Learning to be attentive and aware is also a sound basis for educational learning (Siegel 2007). Mindfulness increases concentration, and students who practice mindfulness are better at focusing and holding awareness. They're also better at relaxing, at reaching appropriate decisions in connection with conflicts, and they're less nervous when taking tests (Napoli et al. 2005).

Social and emotional learning programs in mindfulness can give students better subject results, better moods, greater self-confidence and increased concentration, as well as better social behavior (Weissberg et al. 2011). By practicing mindfulness, children also learn skills that help them to find calm and bring awareness to their inner and outer experiences. One of the greatest advantages of mindfulness is the ability to see things clearly. Clarity helps us to place experiences in their right places, and we become able to respond in a manner that is proportionate to the experience.

Mindfulness Fosters Social Skills

When children have learned to settle themselves and focus through breath awareness, they gradually develop sensory awareness. The next step is to have an eye to how awareness and the body respond to the senses. One of the cornerstones of mindfulness practice is creating clarity of awareness. Our attitudes shape our conduct: if we believe that our impressions, thoughts, and memories are always correct and true, it can lead to frustration and disappointment. If we react emotionally, it's a good idea to withdraw our attention a little, so we can have a little breathing space before drawing a negative conclusion about what's happening or not happening. This makes it easier to see the bigger picture, and respond to it intelligently and compassionately. This perspective helps children connect to themselves (what do I see, feel, and think?) and to others (what do they see, feel and think?). When children begin to see themselves as connected to their environment, they feel less isolated and alone and more empathetic and engaged. They learn to be aware of how their words and deeds affect other people throughout the day.

The Mindfulness Teacher

Teachers who undertake to teach children mindfulness should first participate in several mindfulness courses, and establish and integrate their own practice in everyday life. This applies both to formal and informal practice. We teach primarily by practicing. It's personal, constant practice and experience that we use as the compass for teaching children. Therefore, we should have direct experience of what we teach. It's also inspiring to practice mindfulness together with a group of other adults, and occasionally take lengthier courses and retreats to deepen our practice. Before we commence practicing mindfulness with children, we should make sure to orient parents in what mindfulness practice is, and the purpose of bringing it into their child's everyday life. This gives parents an opportunity to ask questions and find out what their children will experience. Parents will thereby be better able to support mindfulness practice at home.

The following points are important to remember when instituting mindfulness teaching for children:

- The exercises should suit the child and be age-appropriate.
- We should not discuss the child's private feelings or experiences. Mindfulness is not therapy; it's instruction.
- Avoid long, technical explanations about mindfulness, awareness, and the body. Visual, practical demonstrations are often more powerful than the purely verbal.

Thoughts and Feelings Are "Guests" in Our Awareness

The purpose of mindfulness practice is to change our relationship to our thoughts. In doing so, we may find our thoughts change. Through cognitive flexibility we create space for other perspectives in awareness. This form of mindfulness practice helps children to be more conscious of their thoughts and feelings, and to have a sense of their bodies. Mindfulness practice also trains children not to automatically judge a person, object, or experience as good or bad, but instead to meet every situation with interest and see what is special about it. In the same way, children will come to learn that the feelings and thoughts that occupy them are simply passing "guests" in their awareness and not fundamental aspects of themselves. Instead of reacting out of habit to their feelings and thoughts, they learn to choose how to respond to challenges with increased awareness. Children learn to create a mindful "space" between direct emotional reactions and the inappropriate response that often follows. They gain the freedom to respond in a mindful way.

Focused and Receptive Awareness

It is essential to give children a shared language for what it means to be aware. When we ask children to be aware, what exactly are we asking? To be aware of one thing and shut out others? To be aware of a whole range of things simultaneously, for instance a thought, a feeling, and a bodily sense all at once? Or do we want them to shift their awareness from one thing to another? In order to give children clear and precise instructions, we must realize that there are two different forms of awareness: 1) direct, focused awareness and 2) open, receptive awareness.

Direct, focused awareness is awareness focused on a chosen object. This kind of awareness can be described to children using the example of archery, where one tries to hit the red ring in the middle of the target with a bow and arrow. The arrow represents the awareness, and the red ring in the target is the child's chosen object—it might be a book, a game, or his breathing. The child focuses awareness (takes aim) and tries to hit the red ring as well as he can. Sometimes he might miss, while other times he'll hit the bull's-eye, right in the middle. Both experiences are important in the learning process.

Focused awareness means being able to focus awareness on a chosen object for a number of seconds or longer. When a child has first learned to direct her awareness toward a chosen object, the training lies in holding her attention there for longer and longer periods at a time. The child therefore has to learn to be aware of what her attention is directed toward and realize if she has become distracted, in which case she can decide to bring her attention back to the chosen object.

Open, receptive awareness is a broad awareness with primary focus on what is most important in it. The child learns to register what comes and goes in the awareness scene and she doesn't consider these things a distraction, as in focused awareness.

Mindfulness Practice with Children

Remember these three points when introducing mindfulness practice to children:

- Repetition strengthens learning.
- Variation fosters children's interest.
- Actively involve the children (drawing, writing, working with sense activities; practice sitting meditation, body scanning, and visualization).

The following guidelines help to ensure that children have the best possible experience with mindfulness.

> ATMOSPHERE: Try to establish a pleasant and positive mood before starting to practice mindfulness. Make clear to the children why they're practicing it and how it can help them. You may choose to integrate mindfulness as a natural extension of your other teaching. This makes for a more informal practice, in which

there's no separation between exercising mindfulness and other classroom activities.

PRACTICE: A good exercise for children is to practice awareness of breathing (see the first exercise, "Breath," below). Through short breathing meditations the children learn that the breath is the anchor that stabilizes thoughts and feelings. The breath is an important tool for children in many different situations. They can use their breath to calm and comfort themselves when they feel angry or sad.

DISCUSSION: After children have practiced awareness of the breath, discuss how it can be used in daily life. Now is a good opportunity for children to ask questions or ask for help with their practice. It's our responsibility to help children understand their experiences with mindfulness. We can do this by asking questions that bring them back to their own experiences. We're not trying to draw conclusions on their behalf or project our own experiences on to theirs. We're always aware of respecting the child's private space.

USING WHAT WE'VE LEARNED: We try to use what we've learned through mindfulness in the rest of our daily life. Teach children to use situations from their everyday experiences as "mindfulness bells." These "bells" remind us to stop and take note of our breathing, to integrate calm, and be present in everyday events. The list of mindfulness bells could include the ringing of a telephone, a crowing rooster, an ice-cream-truck bell, the ticking of the kitchen clock, or the local church bells ringing.

It's also good to work with mindfulness through other forms of active participation. Children can make pictures, write poems, and do written exercises that describe mindfulness practice in various ways. Each child can have her own notebook in which she collects experiences she has along the way. The book can also be used at home as a journal for mindfulness homework exercises.

Rules for Mindful Behavior

It's helpful to have a clear set of rules for mindful behavior before starting to practice. The following five rules are important during mindfulness practice:

- Speak and behave with kindness and care for others.
- Don't speak when someone else is speaking. Listen with full attention.
- Put your hand up if you want to say something. You can also use a stone; whoever is holding the stone speaks. After speaking, he places the stone in the middle. Then another child is allowed to take the stone and speak.
- Remain quiet during the exercise.
- If you need a break during the exercise, you can sit in the "quiet space" (for example, a chair placed in the corner).

BREATH
———

A good image that can inspire us when we're helping children to find their physical position for mindfulness practice is taken from mountain landscapes: the body as a mountain, the breath as the wind, and awareness as the sky. The body is steady, upright, and relaxed; the breath moves naturally in and out; awareness is either focused on the breath, or open and receptive to what comes and goes as the focus of our attention.

When the children are sitting quietly, say something along these lines: "I'd like you to bring your awareness to your breath. You can pay attention to your breath by putting a hand on your tummy, and feel how your tummy moves in and out with the breath. Try to keep your awareness on your breathing as well as you can. Notice the air that comes in and goes out again, in and out. If your attention wanders off from your breath, it's all right. Just bring it back to breathing in and breathing out, breathing in and breathing out. Your attention will wander off and be full of other thoughts. That's completely okay, because that's what thoughts do. Your job is to bring your attention carefully back to your breathing each time you notice that it's wandered off. Tell yourself it's great that you noticed it and carry on with having your attention on your breathing." (Greenland 2010)

THE JEWEL

This exercise helps children get to know their breathing better. Let each child choose a stone. They can pretend the stone is a beautiful jewel. The children lie on thier backs on pads and each child places a stone on his belly button. Ask the children to notice how the stone moves upward with the in-breath and downward with the out-breath. The children can try to notice the midpoint between breathing in and breathing out. Let the children notice how it feels to let their attention rest in the breathing and in the still space between in-breath and out-breath. Ask the children to notice their breath through the nostrils, and to feel how the air is slightly cool when it comes in and warmer when it goes out again.

THOUGHT PARADE

This exercise helps children connect with their breath and notice how thoughts come and go, as if on a thought parade. They may notice that some thoughts "make a noise" and are colorfully dressed. Other thoughts seem shy and stay in the background, while some go by again and again. When the children realize that they're woven into the parade and are engrossed in thoughts, they're asked to come back onto the sidewalk and, once again, simply watch their thoughts go by. This exercise trains children to observe their thoughts without attaching to them. (Willard 2010)

WALKING MEDITATION

This exercise is a good variation on the sitting-still exercises. Here we learn the ability to be aware while moving. Walk like animals in the forest, who don't frighten other animals and make them run away. This silent, aware walking helps us listen to nature and our surroundings.

Every step is quiet, and with every step we are aware of our bodies and our feet. Breathe in gently and lift your right leg, and notice the feelings in the muscles as they stretch. Carefully begin to put your foot on the ground, first placing the heel down, then the middle of the foot, and finally your toes. Now bring your weight down through the right leg while carefully lifting your left leg off the ground. Notice how your body instinctively knows how to walk, without your having to think about it. Notice how the left heel meets the ground and how the rest of the foot touches the ground again. If your attention moves away, notice how it finds itself and continues with what it was doing. We let the earth carry us and walk without any fixed aim. Walk with this step and with this breathing. Be here and now. Notice how silent our steps are while we walk together. (Willard 2010)

GRATITUDE

In order to bring presence and gratitude into children's consciousness we can use this short gratitude exercise. Ask each child to name three good things that have happened in the course of the last couple of days, or something that they are generally thankful for.

EATING A RAISIN

The raisin exercise helps children to be aware that everything around them has a history. The exercise can be used with many different objects.

Show the children a raisin and ask them where it comes from. Trace all the people who have been in contact with the raisin. You can make a diagram on the chalkboard or on a piece of paper, and write down all the people who've made a contribution to the raisin's being *here*. For example, there's the person who planted the grapevine, the farmworker who harvested the grapes, and the person who dried them and brought them to market. Remember everyone, including the driver from the vineyard, the worker who packed the raisins, the truck driver, the factory workers, the person who put the raisins on the shelf in the store, the checkout person who sold the raisin, and you, who bought the box of raisins. Include the family and friends of all these people: the people who gave them birth and brought them up, and the people who built the truck and plowed the soil. Each child should now choose a person from the raisin story and draw or write a story about this person's contribution to the story. Read the stories aloud to each other or look at the drawings before eating the raisin slowly and with great awareness (Willard 2010).

This exercise can be a step on the way to creating an ethical consciousness and understanding how everything is connected.

CASE STUDY

The Minute: An Exercise in Silence in the Classroom

Martin Ammentorp, teacher, Denmark: I began a personal meditation practice based on the breath about twenty years ago. I increased my consciousness about what breathing, concentration, and inner peace mean for a person's well-being, presence, and awareness. For a long time I wanted to integrate my practice into my daily work with students and student teachers. Through my work in the music department, I had always used concentration exercises together with consciousness of deep breathing in my teaching.

What I undertake with the students is a breathing space in the middle of a hectic day of school. A moment when we take a break together, relax, and try to engage in the present moment. It gives the students the experience that "doing nothing" can be worthwhile and experiencing that together can be very special.

In all my classes, music, English, and math, I now use The Minute. The students are instructed to sit comfortably and straight, and to shut their eyes. No talking, no other contact with classmates. I now count down slowly, $5 - 4 - 3 - 2 - 1 - 0$. Now there should be silence in class for one full minute.

At first some of the kids reacted with noise, laughing, or coughing; others fidgeted in their chairs, tried to poke a classmate, or opened their eyes to wink at their friends. I ignored all this, didn't mention it, and after a while they settled down. I ask them to notice their breathing—just to notice it. Sometimes I ask them to notice the sensations in their noses when they breathe in.

When The Minute works without reactions or interruptions, the exercise can be prolonged for two, three, or four minutes. On other occasions we listen in silence to a bell that I have in the classroom.

My experience is that teaching after doing this exercise brings renewed energy. The students have a renewed freshness and enter into their tasks with better concentration. I also use The Minute with teacher trainees, and I get positive feedback, not only from their own personal experience but also from their applying it in the classroom. It's wonderful for me to meet a trainee teacher who tells me she has tried the exercise with a difficult and restless class and found her students much better able to concentrate afterward.

My own students have told me: "It's so nice to be so quiet together." "It's so great to do nothing." "I can concentrate better now." These are just their statements. I can see with my own eyes their relaxed faces, their little smiles, and their peaceful breathing.

CHAPTER 12

What Mindfulness Is Not

WHEN MINDFULNESS IS INTRODUCED into a school or into a classroom or other learning environment, it must be done with a clear understanding of what is expected so that it doesn't accidentally produce more stress rather than less! In the worst case, mindfulness can be used to cover structural or contextual problems in a given educational environment. Mindfulness can complement and inspire other structural changes, but shouldn't be used as something that can take the place of other needed changes. In order to fully understand what mindfulness can contribute to a learning environment, it's helpful to explain that there are several things mindfulness is *not*.

Mindfulness is not:
1. Something that oversteps private boundaries
2. Therapy rather than a teaching
3. Retraumatizing
4. Mandatory
5. Religion
6. Self-centered with no engagement with society

Not Overstepping Private Boundaries
Sometimes, through mindfulness practice, we can accidentally overstep private boundaries. Therefore it's important that participants set

limits for the private realm. This is especially important if the practice is introduced into the workplace. We must take care to understand and respect the boundaries that separate our professional, personal, and private fields.

The professional field is built up through training and specialized experience. It contains the teacher's knowledge and insight concerning the different theories, methods, terminology, and culture surrounding her subject.

The personal field is the way in which we personally transmit our subject. The personal field means that people with the same background may accomplish the same task in different ways. If we had no personal field, we'd be like automatons. The personal field is constructed from the distinguishing traits we bring to our work and our life.

The private field represents those sides of ourselves we don't bring into the workplace, and the aspects we keep to ourselves. It can be parts of our personality or concrete knowledge that we don't share.

In working life we move within the professional and personal fields (the two outer circles), whereas in private life we move within the personal and private fields (the two inner circles). It's impossible to only place things in relation to one of the fields. For example, June is the mother of two children, and that's a private affair. But June uses the knowledge she's gained from being a mother in her work. June's colleagues and coworkers know that she has two children; they also know their names, how old they are, how much June loves them, and perhaps whether the children have any special difficulties. But there will always be a wide range of things concerning June's children that she keeps within the private field.

As teachers, it's important that we protect our private field in our work situation. We must be our own border guards and know where our boundaries lie. How much do we invite a colleague to open up to

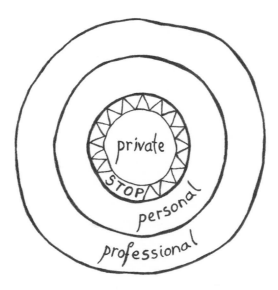

FIGURE 14:1. The personal and the professional fields belong to our working lives. The boundaries surrounding our private fields must be strictly adhered to.

us with regard to our own boundaries? If we're too open, it can lead to having knowledge about another that goes beyond our own private boundaries. When we practice mindfulness, it's important that we make use of our inner border guard when we confront something that can be private, such as feelings, thoughts, bodily sensations, and the way we are in relation to the world.

Teaching, Not Therapy

The mindfulness teacher is not a therapist, and it's not the intention that mindfulness teaching should become therapy. In therapy, a person's emotional challenges are laid bare, often with the primary aim that the therapist should help the person. Education is characterized, on the other hand, as a relationship in which the teacher sets up opportunities for learning to take place. If a teacher has emotional challenges it's important not to invite a confessional mood in connection with mindfulness practice. We sympathize with emotional difficulties not by commenting on them, but by listening consciously without making judgments.

Not Retraumatizing

People with traumas that have not been worked through can, through the mindfulness mechanism of exposure, come into contact with the unmanageable powerlessness that underlies the trauma. If such an unresolved trauma is exposed without the person being able to cope with the situation, there's a risk of retraumatizing. Sitting mindfully can, for some participants, cause them to confront both uncertainty and their own limits. When mindfulness is practiced, we lay ourselves open, and therefore are vulnerable to experiencing both life's cheerful and disheartening sides. It can be difficult to be present for long periods in the here and now with acceptance and insight, and it can certainly test the participant's limits.

It's important to be aware that we're good enough as we are. It's also important that mindfulness teaching must not challenge participants to practice for longer periods at a time than the participant can tolerate. In this way we can try to ensure that people are not challenged beyond their capabilities. Finally, it's important that the mindfulness teacher has a long experience of practice behind her, so that her teaching can be a source of good advice.

Allowing Exemption

If we wish to introduce mindfulness in an educational setting, everyone who participates should do so willingly. Mindfulness practice shouldn't be compulsory for anyone. Mindfulness is founded on personal motivation. Teachers not wishing to take part in the practice because of psychological or ideological reasons must be allowed to exempt themselves.

Not a Religion

Mindfulness isn't a religion, but a practice based on research. It's a universal mode for being aware in a way that everyone can practice, regardless of whether they have any religious affiliation or not. We must not blindly have faith in the practice and its effects, but rather trust our own experiences. In mindfulness we don't work with a supernatural world or a concept of the divine that influences our conduct.

Not Self-Centered or Unengaged with Society

Although we're conscious of the thoughts, feelings, and senses that arise in our awareness, mindfulness should not become a self-centered practice. It's quite the reverse. The intention is that we should practice so as to take responsibility for our own behavior, so we can best create the optimum learning environment. Mindfulness is not about personal success, and it's not a method to get ahead in the world at the expense of others. If we forget the perspective of interbeing, self-centeredness begins to play tricks. Mindfulness isn't a method for gaining personal power. The intention is to create happiness and reduce pain. Achieving inner peace and contentment with mindfulness shouldn't make us so complacent that we forget to think about other people's suffering. Instead, mindfulness encourages us all to engage ourselves in the mutual creation of a better future.

CHAPTER 13
The Insights of Mindfulness

The practice of mindfulness reveals a range of important existential insights. In previous chapters we've described how anger can be transformed into kindness, and how we can learn to alter our habitual reactions to conscious responses. The following insights can inspire us to contemplate ourselves further.

1. Alienation versus interbeing
2. Pain versus suffering
3. Desire versus generosity
4. Permanence versus change

Contemplation is a form of concentrated deepening, which fosters insight and wisdom. The first insight on alienation versus interbeing can be seen as the fundamental suffering in the human being. The conviction that we're permanent, separate individuals leads us to believe that we don't have enough and that we're never good enough. This leads us to become full of the sense of having to strive and make our mark. The experience of being alienated from and indifferent to the world creates desire, anxiety, and anger. It's the basis for suffering in us and in the world.

Something Missing

Nikolaj: When I was a teenager, I was a semiprofessional soccer player. I was driven to refine my technique, get in excellent physical condition, and increase my understanding of the game so I could improve and win our games. I wanted mastery over myself. At the same time, my interest in heavy metal music grew stronger than my career as a soccer player. When I look back at that time, I can see that I used my work as a rock singer and songwriter to try to clarify and express existential challenges. I lived in high gear with soccer, music, and parties. Even though I kept on raising the bar for performing better and partying more, I often felt a lurking sense of dissatisfaction. In time I grew sick of this feeling, and I began to be interested in psychological and philosophical practices that could minimize my existential dissatisfaction. These were steps in the right direction, but these practices were mostly about self-mastery. I never felt completely satisfied. No matter how perfectly I mastered something, something was always missing. But what was it?

In 1999 I read Thich Nhat Hanh's commentary on the Diamond Sutra (Nhat Hanh 1992). Reading this bowled me over. Over and over I reread this sentence: "If a bodhisattva holds on to the idea that a self, a person, a living being, or a life span exists, that person is not an authentic bodhisattva." What did this mean? I'd been working for years to improve myself, only to learn that there was no such thing as a self? I was really shaken. At the same time, I felt incredibly liberated, as if a burden had been lifted from me. My drive to master myself now found itself within a wider context. I went from a feeling of being alienated from the world to a greater experience of interbeing. I experienced a sense of belonging in the world, and this created profound joy, and an increased wish to help and contribute.

Alienation versus Interbeing

When we're mindful, we identify less with our thoughts and feelings. Freed from our habitual inner turmoil, we experience a higher degree of interbeing and connection to our environment. We no longer seek to compete with others. We don't feel we have to defend ourselves, or that we have to achieve something in order to be good enough. The fundamental experience of interbeing makes us more at ease. The deep-seated feeling of being in a state of lack becomes a feeling of abundance that can be shared with others.

Pain versus Suffering

Disappointment, loneliness, sickness, loss, and death are unavoidable parts of life. This is the pain of life. At the same time, we can conduct ourselves in ways that either alleviate life's pain or aggravate it. When we aggravate pain, it becomes suffering. Suffering is the extra aggravation we inflict on top of pain. We may try to soothe pain temporarily through distractions such as unhealthy eating, gossip, complaining, mindless entertainment, substance abuse, and shopping. These things may bring us temporary relief, but they cause more suffering in the long run.

Through mindfulness practice we try to alleviate the pain. We do this by meeting our pain with acceptance and compassion, by allowing ourselves to be one with our breathing and by being grateful for what we have. When we've reconciled ourselves with the situation, we may get an insight that reveals appropriate strategies to meet the challenges. Mindfulness alleviates our pain by putting in its place a greater experience of interbeing.

Desire versus Generosity

There are healthy desires and there are unhealthy desires. Unhealthy desires are based on ignorance and greed. They create anxiety, material craving, self-centeredness, and discontent, and can lead to dependency and addiction. But we can practice stopping and choosing whether to hang on to these desires or let them go. Healthy desires create happiness, care for others, integrity, and generosity. Healthy desires are based on wisdom and compassion, and they make it possible for us to feed our families, care for our children and ourselves, and enhance our work, our community, and ourselves.

Learning to recognize the difference between the two types of desire is an important task. In order to transform unhealthy desires, we learn to notice how they work in our own bodies and minds. When we feel a powerful desire for something, it's usually followed by an emotional and physical tension. Our awareness is full of what we desire and our focus is on something in the future. When we're lost in desire, we don't think of other people, but are primarily focused on our own needs. Through mindfulness we can watch our desires come and go without being caught by them or judging them.

Permanence versus Change

When we observe our thoughts and feelings with an attitude of disengagement, we notice that thoughts and feelings change quickly. They're just like all other things; everything has the nature of changing. This insight works against disappointment and enlarges our peace of mind. We don't try to hold on to things that change. As teachers, we have a special opportunity to witness changes close up, since children grow and change quickly. We're often surprised after summer vacation when we see how much the children have changed. We see that they've grown taller, or more articulate, or more spirited.

Mindfulness Exercise
CONTEMPLATION

We can use this exercise to broaden our basic mindfulness practice after it's well established.

1. After we've worked with the basic mindfulness practice, we write down the most important questions in our life on a piece of paper. (We may also choose to pose a question in connection with one of the insights in this chapter.)

2. We ask the question and are present with it in silence. We don't try to answer the question; just to be one with it and remain open to the insights that may come.

3. We return to basic practice when we're either too distracted or too eager to find an answer to the question.

The insight that life is unpredictable and changeable can alter the way we experience our lives and the way we live. We're less shocked and disappointed when something changes, and we're more able to grasp the unfolding possibilities of any situation, just like the man in the following story.

The Tigers

A man met a tiger while out for a walk. The tiger chased him over a cliff. As the man fell over the cliff, he managed to grab a root sticking out of the mountainside. Far below, he saw another tiger, hoping to catch and eat him. The man looked up and saw the first hungry tiger. Then there appeared two mice who began to nibble at the root he was holding on to. In that moment, the man saw a delicious strawberry, and as he held onto the root with one hand, he picked the strawberry with the other. Ah! How good that strawberry tasted (Rosenberg 2004).

CHAPTER 14
Revolution of Silence

THE GREAT FOCUS ON INDIVIDUALITY in Western culture stands in opposition to the fact that in previous eras we perceived ourselves as a small part of a greater whole. In ancient times, humankind had a completely different relationship to the self. Most people believed they were part of a clan, or, as in ancient Greece, part of a greater cosmic unity. This meant that the individual developed herself in relation to something other than herself.

Social pathologies are illnesses that manifest societally. The symptoms of social pathologies show that changes in structure and values can clearly be seen in the individual's psyche and relationship to himself. For instance, the French sociologist Alain Ehrenberg describes how a rise in depression and the increased use of antidepressants in our society is caused by a disintegration of society's support for a person to be himself. In this culture of self-realization one is obliged to develop oneself and exploit one's potentials as an individual. The problem with this culture of self-realization is that it takes place on the foundation of individuality and disconnection. This leads to self-centeredness, anxiety, and the feeling that we're constantly lacking something. If our culture is going to overcome these tendencies toward sickness, we must establish another perspective as the basis for our development as individuals and as a society.

Interbeing as a Basis for Development

As we described at the beginning of this book, the meditative intention with mindfulness practice changes over a period of time from mastery of the self to selflessness. Through continued practice over a period of time, there comes about a self-transcendent acknowledgment that throws new light on existence. We go from longing to belonging; from a basic yearning to a feeling of being at home in the world. Mindfulness practice helps us to change our experience of being in a state of lack and longing, to being in a state of abundance that can make others happy too. At the same time, through compassion and openness, we shatter the sense of isolation and alienation. Self-transcendence can take the place of isolation, and the experience of interbeing accompanies it.

As Leonard Cohen sings in "Anthem," "There's a crack in everything; that's how the light gets in." The "crack" is self-transcendence—that's what allows the light in. The crack can be our gateway to selflessness. If we don't advance our practice beyond self-mastery, we run the risk that we'll constantly experience a state of loss. In such a state we continue to hanker after something that can only be satisfied through selflessness. The development potential for mindfulness lies in having a deeper perspective—the perspective that our practice can lead to an experience of self-transcendence and selflessness. Korean Zen teachers give the following picture of how self-absorption can be transcended.

The Beautiful Island

We're on a remote desert island, but we believe that another person is also living there. We search everywhere, going over the island with a fine-toothed comb, from one end to the other. Finally, we realize that no one else is there. In the same instant, we become conscious that the island is extraordinarily beautiful (Rosenberg 2004).

The Revolution of Silence

Silence has become like a foreign language to us. We're full of inner unrest and intrusive thoughts that grow more evident with outer quiet. Therefore, many of us flee from our own company by surrounding ourselves with the Internet, cell phones, and TV sets. We can't endure silence because we're full of inner interference from our thoughts and feelings. Perhaps silence also reminds us of the loneliness of death.

Life is given to us on loan, and sooner or later the loan will be called in. But it can be difficult to look this fact in the eye. To avoid confronting anxiety, insufficiency, and the knowledge of our own death, we live through defense mechanisms, and we try to dull our pain with junk food, mindless entertainment, substance abuse, and excessive shopping. These things are quick, hedonistic fixes that create more suffering in the long run.

We also consume through our sense impressions. There is some connection between interest in violent entertainment and the potential to commit violent acts (Huismann 2006). Through mindfulness practice we can train our awareness to keep watch over our sense gateways, or sense organs. Our "watchmen" must be ready to evaluate what is healthy and what is poisonous to consume, and also what is appropriate to contribute to a situation. Our basic intention in life also has a great influence on our relationship to silence. If our intention is driven by unhealthy desires, it brings suffering in the form of inner unrest, self-centeredness, and dissatisfaction. This suffering stands in the way of silence and interbeing.

Interbeing Approaches in Silence

The intention of setting in motion an inner silent revolution is to help people to feel more comfortable and be on more intimate terms with silence. Silence can be the signpost to insight and experiences of interbeing.

The silence of this revolution isn't defined by the absence of outer sound, but by the presence of inner silence. This is a silence in which thoughts and feelings grow quiet through a compassionate, accepting state of being. When inner silence arises, feelings of lack and detachment fall away and interbeing approaches. An environment where there's outer silence can help us calm the inner turmoil which over time can be transformed into inner silence.

We can have outer silence when we take part in a retreat. On a retreat we retire for a time to deepen our practice, free from everyday worries and concerns and the demands of work. On retreat we spend some days in silence when we can shift focus and give ourselves time to be present. Everything is arranged so that we may deepen our mindfulness practice. Retreats are held in surroundings where outer disturbances are reduced, and where we have the opportunity to be silent ourselves. In the silence we can more easily experience our connectedness as well as our relationship to loneliness, death, and the impermanence of all things.

Being on intimate terms with silence is an essential capacity in the educational world. If we can make ourselves silent, it's easier to put ourselves in the child's place and see what effects we have on her and the learning situation. It's also easier to be grateful for the good that exists, and see possible ways for dealing with obstacles. When we create inner silence, our inappropriate thoughts and feelings don't stand in our way. On the contrary, promoting inner calm and silence can change a basic experience of being in a state of lack to one of abundance. This abundance strengthens the teacher, the children, and society.

CASE STUDY FROM KINDERGARTEN
Mindfulness in Everyday Work

Dorte Them-Møller, leader, open-air kindergarten, Denmark

In our kindergarten, we work consciously with how we are in our interactions with the children; we train ourselves to be present and listen to the child so as to adapt ourselves to their needs and capacities. Through this awareness and reflection we work consciously with mood and pace. The mood is an important influence on what happens around us, and the possibilities that we create, and so is being conscious of our pace throughout the course of the day. There are moments when we are on 120 percent and moments when we are on 70 percent.

The same applies to the children. We strive to be in small groups with the children, to maintain calm and presence, to create space for the individual child to be part of the interplay. However, we live in a time when there are fewer staff members, and it's frustrating for the staff to feel that there isn't enough time to really be present and interact fruitfully with the children. The staff feel that they're pressed to the limit. They are "on" more often and for longer periods. For these reasons I've introduced mindfulness to give the staff a tool to counter some of the pressure in their work. All staff members are offered the opportunity to practice mindfulness twice a week for fifteen minutes. The entire faculty has had a short introductory course in mindfulness, and there's been some good feedback from having had time for this. The training is optional, but time is set aside in the daily schedule for it, and everyone knows they have the opportunity to practice mindfulness on any given day.

In our educational work, we work on relationships, which demands that coworkers be present in the moment. They develop skills in listening, acknowledging, using their senses, and becoming spatially aware. It increases the fun they have with the children and with each other. I believe that mindfulness is a superb tool to have available to create balance in a person.

Quotes from Kindergarten Staff Members

- Practicing mindfulness is something I look forward to. It generates calm in mind and body, and it's a place of refuge. For a few minutes afterward I may still feel drowsy, but then it's as though I've taken something that is energy-giving. You become full of new energy.

- I feel I have abundance, I become more creative, and it gives me more happiness and calm. I don't notice it as I practice mindfulness, but it's the result of practicing mindfulness. I enjoy the break and the calm—calm in body and mind.

- I love having mindfulness. I can use mindfulness to keep my attention on a problematic situation, and through it find new ideas and solutions.

Teachers aren't the only people who suffer from the growing stress in society. Children are also tormented by noise and disturbance. Children don't have the option to choose another way of life. Therefore, it's our responsibility to give them a chance to be on easy terms with silence and presence. As one of the students expressed in the case history "The Minute," "It's so nice to be so quiet together." The way we bring up and help shape the individual child has great consequences not only for that child but also for hundreds, perhaps thousands of people the child will meet in her future. In light of this, rearing children wisely is one of society's important tasks.

In order for teachers to function as the superstars they are, they must have the opportunity to be at ease with silence and interbeing. And for that, mindfulness is an invaluable support. Listen to the pin drop.

The trees fall silent
Darkness among the tree trunks
The woodpecker knocks
—Didde Flor Rotne

APPENDIX 1
The Somatic Markers

MINDFULNESS STRENGTHENS OUR CAPACITY for something called interoception—sensitivity to internal stimuli (Lutz et al 2008; Brefcynski-Lewis et al 2007). When we lose contact with our body and breathing, we become more vulnerable to stress and burnout because we fail to notice the stress symptoms. It's important therefore for teachers to train themselves to notice and understand the meaning of the physical symptoms. This applies not least to interpersonal situations that can be stressful. The somatic markers—physical symptoms—are important signals from the body, which explain how the feelings as perceived in the body can give valuable indications for decision making.

The physical signals function as messengers for the feelings. In a situation where we have to make a choice, before we begin to weigh the pros and cons, the somatic marker works as a physical indication. It functions through its connection to the amygdala as an automatic alarm that helps us to focus on the possible dangers connected with choosing an option, including the possible dangers that might result in the long term from a choice that gives an instant profit (Damasio 2001). The somatic marker can also be positive, working automatically to draw us toward a definite choice that's bound to mental images of a desirable future situation and to our reward mechanism. Reward mechanisms are included in the neurotransmitter nuclei in the brain stem—for instance, those that secrete dopamine, noradrenalin, and serotonin—and in the

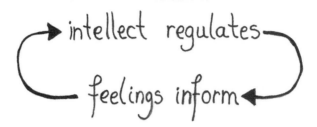

FIGURE 3:3. The feelings can be seen as important messengers that the intellect must interpret and regulate. We can become aware of these messengers through bodily signals (somatic markers).

connections to the somatic-sensory cortical areas where former and current physical conditions are continuously represented. These bodily signals can also mislead us. Therefore it's important that we train ourselves to interpret them correctly.

There are two preconditions for being able to employ the somatic marker signals in such a way that decision-making processes can be more effective and precise.

The first precondition is that we can become aware of them. If we're unable to notice the physical signals that precede our considerations during a decision-making process, we can't make proper use of them. But if we can take notice of our bodily signals, they can be used either by reacting intuitively to them or by entering into a process of reflection.

The second precondition is that we can interpret and manage the somatic markers. If we notice an unfamiliar bodily signal, it can't be of any practical use until we can interpret it and know how to use it.

Coherence

Research shows a connection between the heart's emotional system and the brain's limbic system. In recent decades, research has demonstrated that the abdominal-intestinal system and the heart have their own network of thousands of neurons that function as "little brains" in the body (Servan-Schreiber 2004). These localized brains are able to have their own senses and even transform themselves as a result of their experiences. The connection between these little brains and the emotional limbic brain goes through the autonomic peripheral nervous system, which is the part of the nervous system that regulates all organ functions outside of human consciousness and beyond the reach of the will.

The autonomic nervous system comprises two parts that both connect the bodily organs with nerves from the emotional brain. The sympathetic part releases adrenalin and noradrenalin. It directs the fight-or-flight reactions, and its activity causes the heart rhythm to increase. The parasympathetic part releases the neurotransmitter acetylcholine, which can bring relaxation and calm. Its activity can put a brake on the rhythm of the heart. In states of stress, anxiety, depression, or anger, the variability of the heart rhythm becomes unregulated and chaotic. In states of well-being, empathy, and gratitude, this variability becomes "coherent"—that is, the changes between rising and falling heart rhythms become regulated. If the person doesn't maintain the

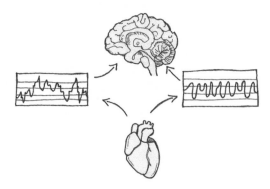

FIGURE 5:1. This illustration shows the means by which brain and heart mutually affect the heart rhythm. The left-hand graph shows a chaotic pulse and the right shows an example of a coherent pulse.

parasympathetic system's capacity to put a brake on the heart rhythm, the system shrivels like an unused muscle. Thus we can see that the state of heart coherence, with its impact on the natural variability of blood pressure and breathing, is a central point from which to manage and avoid stress.

Stress: When the Amygdala Runs Wild

The amygdala is located in the temporal lobes of the limbic system and it registers danger. It affects the hypothalamus, which tries to hold the stress-affected system in balance. The hypothalamus instructs the suprarenal glands to release more cortisol to cope with the energy loss resulting from a pressured situation (see figure 6:1.). Cortisol slows down the immune system, the ability to learn, and the ability to relax. This reaction is useful in short bursts, when we have to increase our performance in the short term. It's as though cortisol says, Forget about learning new stuff, forget about fighting off sickness, and forget about relaxing. This is an emergency! (Gerhardt 2005). Cortisol reduces fat and proteins to create more energy, thereby putting other systems temporarily on hold.

When the crisis is past, the cortisol is gradually taken up by its receptors or dissolved by enzymes, and the body returns to its normal functions. But if the stress continues and high levels of cortisol remain in the body, it can affect the immune system's lymphocytes, making them less responsive, finally breaking them down, and preventing new ones from developing. If cortisol levels remain high, the cortisol receptors can shut down, and make the hippocampus less cortisol-sensitive and less able to give feedback to the hypothalamus to let it know to stop further cortisol production. Without this feedback, the stress responses remain in place, with cortisol continuing to be pumped

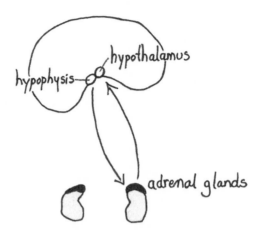

FIGURE 6:1. The HPA axis (hypothalamic-pituitary-adrenal axis) shows the physiological rotation in which the hypothalamus releases a stress response as a reaction to stressful experiences. The hypothalamus activates the hypophysis (pituitary gland), which in turn activates the adrenal (suprarenal) glands. This causes the adrenal glands to produce extra cortisol to give the body increased energy to prepare it to deal with the stress. This puts other systems on hold while the cortisol does its work.

into the system. This can mean that too much glutamate, an important neurotransmitter, is sent to the hippocampus, which can create neuron loss, leading to possible loss of function that manifests in memory loss and learning difficulties. The amygdala is activated by cortisol and continues releasing noradrenalin, which in turn releases more cortisol. Thus energy levels increase. Only the prefrontal cortex—the frontal lobes—has the capacity to control the amygdala. But if the stress continues, the neurotransmitters, the brain's motive power, reduce activity. Dopamine and serotonin levels drop under these conditions. Dopamine and serotonin are, like endorphins, neurotransmitters that are closely linked with feelings of happiness and well-being. Chronic stress reactions inhibit endorphin activity.

Mindfulness Creates Density in the Brain's Gray Matter

The brain changes when we practice mindfulness. In an experiment, twenty people with a regular, long-term practice of meditation were tested for thickening of the cerebral cortex through an MRI (magnetic resonance imaging) scan. The results of the tests showed that the brain areas associated with interoception, awareness, and sensory information processing were substantially thicker in people who had a long-established meditation practice, compared with the control group. The thickness of the gray matter was also defined in relation to the degree of meditation practice (Lazar et al. 2005). The increased thickness that indicates that many synaptic connections have been created are, among other things, registered in the spinal marrow that controls the breath and heart rhythm, as well as in the frontal lobes with reference to the capacity for interoception (Westergaard-Poulsen et al. 2009). The tests show similarly that mindfulness fosters the capacity for interoception (Lutz et al. 2008). In recent years an experiment has been undertaken that shows the increased thickness of the brain structure in connection with mindfulness meditation. Among other things one can show that mindfulness practice creates a continuous, steady concentration. The strengthened concentration is intentional and means that we can control what our awareness is focused upon (Lutz et al. 2008, 2009).

APPENDIX 5
Mirror Neurons

The nerve cells in the brain that can direct a certain event (for example, an action or feeling) but that also become active when observing another person's action or feeling are called mirror neurons (Rizzolatti et al. 2002, 2008). This resonance happens spontaneously without our having to think about it. Mirror resonance gives us the ability to know what's happening in the person whom we observe. This sensation constitutes an important basis for decision making in the observer. Mirror resonance also explains how both stress and well-being, as well as other moods and feelings, are spread.

Research with monkeys has shown that action neurons and movement neurons fired off their signals when a monkey reached for a peanut on a tray. Researchers had localized the action and movement neurons, and could follow their activity. They could also see that when the monkey saw another monkey reach for a peanut on the tray, his action neurons also fired off. Seeing an action undertaken by another monkey activated the monkey's own neurobiological program. These mirror neurons' reflection activity is set off through watching another's actions; they are also activated by noise. If the peanut were wrapped in paper, the rustling of the paper activated the action neurons.

Then a monkey was allowed to see a nut, and following this, a research assistant set a plate in front of the nut so it couldn't be seen. When another monkey reached for the nut, the first monkey could

FIGURE 7:1. The illustration shows how watching another monkey grab a nut fires off the monkey's action neurons.

see how the other's arm vanished behind the partition. The monkey couldn't see the actual grab, but his action neurons "knew" what had happened. The mirror cell that had stored the program for the whole nut-grabbing event fired off its signal, even though it could only have had information about a part of the action sequence (Umiltà et al. 2001).

The research team looked at human mirror neurons using an MRI scanner. Here one could observe the same phenomenon. When a person saw another's actions, the same action neurons were activated in the watcher as in the person watched, as if the watcher had performed the same action. Moreover, it was also discovered that if the person imagined performing the action, the action neurons fired off their signals then too. It was found that human mirror neurons can also complete the entire sequence of a scene of which only parts have been observed. This phenomenon can be seen in football teams, in which the players know and anticipate each other's behavior patterns, which possibly helps explain the neuropsychology behind intuition. The fact that mirror neurons can make observed parts of a scene into a possible whole sequence is not only relevant to the progress of action but also to feelings and impressions.

When someone enters into our field of vision, a neurobiological resonance is activated in us, whether we want it to be or not. The other person's behavior, such as eye contact, demeanor, or body language summons up reactions in us. Mirror neurons fire off signals when we plan or perform an action, and they fire off signals, too, when we observe or imagine an activity. The action neurons prepare us to act, and they are connected to nerve cells in the gyrus cinguli (basis for sense of life), amygdala (anxiety feelings), and insula (charting the physical state). These give information to the physical body about how it will feel to perform the action (Bauer 2012).

Bibliography

Aron, A., Aron, E. N. and Smollan, D. (1992) "Inclusion of the Other in the Self Scale and the Structure of Interpersonal Closeness." *Journal of Personality and Social Psychology*, 63: 596–612.

Baer, R. A. (2010) *Assessing Mindfulness and Acceptance Processes in Clients: Illuminating the Theory and Practice of Change.* Oakland, CA: New Harbinger Publications.

Barefoot, W. (1985) "The Health Consequences of Hostility. Chesney et al., eds. *Anger and Hostility in Cardiovascular and Behavioral Disorder.* New York, NY: McGraw-Hill.

Bartel, C. and Saavedra, R. (2000) "The Collective Construction of Work Group Moods." *Administrative Science Quarterly*, 45: 187–231.

Batson, D., Ahmed, N., Lishner, D. A., and Tsang, J. (2002) "Empathy and Altruism." Snyder, C. R. and Lopez, S. J., eds. *Handbook of Positive Psychology.* New York, NY: Oxford University Press, USA.

Bauer, J. (2012) *Why I Feel What You Feel. Intuitive Communication and the Secret of Mirror Neurons.* Seattle, WA: AmazonCrossing.

Benson, H. (2000). *The Relaxation Response.* New York, NY: Harper Torch.

Berkman, L. (1992) "Emotional Support and Survival after Myocardial Infarction." *Annals of Internal Medicine*; 117: 1003–1009.

Brefcynski-Lewis, J. A., Lutz, A., Schaefer, H. S., Levinson, D. B., and Davidson, R. J. (2007) "Neural Correlates of Attentional Expertise in Long-Term Meditation Practitioners." *Proceedings of the National Academy of Sciences of the United States of America*, 104: 11,483–11,488.

Bucay, J. (2013) *Let Me Tell You a Story: A New Approach to Healing through the Art of Storytelling.* New York, NY: Europa Editions.

Carmody, J. and Baer, R. A. (2008) "Relationships between Mindfulness Practice and Levels of Mindfulness, Medical and Psychological Symptoms and Well-Being in a Mindfulness-Based Stress Reduction Program." *Journal of Behavioural Medicine*, 31: 23–33.

Cialdini, R. B., Brown, S. L., et al. (1997) "Reinterpreting the Empathy-Altruism Relationship: When One into One Equals Oneness." *Journal of Personality and Social Psychology*, 73: 481–494.

Covey, S. R. (2005). *The 8th Habit: From Effectiveness to Greatness*. New York, NY: Free Press.

Damasio, A. (2005) *Descartes' Error: Emotion, Reason, and the Human Brain*. New York, NY: Penguin Books.

Darley, M. D. and Batson, D. (1973) "From Jerusalem to Jericho: A Study of Situational and Dispositional Variables in Helping Behavior." *Journal of Personality and Social Psychology*, 27: 100–108.

Darwin, C. (1872/1998) *The Expression of the Emotions in Man and Animals*. London: John Murray.

Davidson, R. J., Putnam, K. M., and Larson, C. L. (2000) "Dysfunctional in the Neural Circuitry of Emotion Regulation? A Possible Prelude to Violence." *Science*, 289: 591–594.

Davidson, R., Kabat-Zinn, J., Schumacher, J., Rosenkranz, M., Muller, D., Santorelli, S.F., Urbanowski, F., Harrington, A., Bonus, K., and Sheridan, J. F. (2003). "Alterations in Brain and Immune Function Produced by Mindfulness Meditation." *Psychosomatic Medicine*, 65: 564–570.

Diener, E. and Seligman, M. E. P. (2002) "Very Happy People." *Psychological Science*, 13: 81–84.

Einstein, A. (2000) *The Expanded Quotable Einstein*. Calaprice, A., eds. Princeton, NJ: Princeton University Press.

Eisenberg, N. (2002) *Empathy-Related Emotional Responses, Altruism, and Their Socialization*. Davidson, R.J. and Harrington, A., eds. *Visions of Compassion*. New York, NY: Oxford University Press, USA.

Ekman, P. (2003) *Emotions Revealed: Recognizing Faces and Feelings to Improve Communication and Emotional Life*. New York, NY: Times Books.

Emmons, R. A. and McCullough, M. E. (2003) "Counting Blessings Versus Burdens: An Experimental Investigation of Gratitude and Subjective Well-Being in Daily Life." *Journal of Personality and Social Psychology*, 84: 377–389.

Fredrickson, B. L. (1998) "What Good Are Positive Emotions?" *Review of General Psychology*, 2: 300–319.

Fredrickson, B. L., Cohn, M. A., Coffey, K. A., Pek, J., and Finkel, S. M. (2008) "Open Hearts Build Lives: Positive Emotions, Induced through Loving-Kindness Meditation, Build Consequential Personal Resources." *Journal of Personality and Social Psychology*, 95: 1045–1062.

Fredrickson, B. L. (2009) *Positivity: Groundbreaking Research Reveals How to Embrace the Hidden Strength of Positive Emotions, Overcome Negativity, and Thrive.* New York, NY: Crown Archetype.

Friedman, H. S. and Riggio, R. E. (1981) "Effect of Individual Differences in Nonverbal Expressiveness on Transmission of Emotion." *Journal of Nonverbal Behavior*, 6: 96-104.

Fulton, P. R. and Siegel, R. D. (2005) "Buddhist and Western Psychology: Seeking Common Ground." Germer, C. K., Siegel, R. D., and Fulton, P. R., eds. *Mindfulness and Psychotherapy.* New York, NY: Guilford Press.

Goldberg, E. (2009) *The New Executive Brain: Frontal Lobes in a Complex World.* New York, NY: Oxford University Press, USA.

Goleman, D. (2004) *Destructive Emotions: A Scientific Dialogue with the Dalai Lama.* New York, NY: Bantam.

Greenland, K. S. (2010) *The Mindful Child.* New York, NY: Free Press.

Harris, M. J. and Rosenthal, R. (1985) "Mediation of Interpersonal Expectancy Effects: 31 Meta-Analyses." *Psychological Bulletin*, 97: 363–386.

Hatfield, E., Cacioppo, J. T., and Rapson, R. L. (1994) *Emotional Contagion.* New York, NY: Cambridge University Press.

Hattie, J. (2009) *Visible Learning: A Synthesis of Over 800 Meta-Analyses Relating to Archievement.* New York, NY: Routledge.

Henriques, J. B. and Davidson, R. J. (1997) "Brain Electrical Asymmetries During Cognitive Task Performance in Depressed and Nondepressed Subjects." *Biological Psychiatry*, 42: 1039–1050.

Hokanson, J. E. (1962) "The Effect of Status, Type of Frustation and Aggression on Vascular Process." *Journal of Abnormal and Social Psychology*, 65: 232–237.

Huismann, L. P and Taylor, L. D. (2006) "The Role of Media Violence in Violent Behaviour." *Annual Review of Public Health*, 27: 393–415.

Isen, A. M. and Levin, P. F. (1972) "Effect of Feeling Good on Helping: Cookies and Kindness." *Journal of Personality and Social Psychology*, 21: 382–388.

Isen, A. M., Clark, M., and Schwartz, M. F. (1976) "Duration of the Effect of Good Mood on Helping: Footprints on the Sands of Time." *Journal of Personality and Social Psychology*, 34: 385–393.

Isen, A. M. (1987) "Positive Affect, Cognitive Processes, and Social Behaviour." *Advances in Experimental Social Psychology*, 20: 203–253.

Kabat-Zinn, J. (2003) Mindfulness-Based Interventions in Context: Past, Present, and Future." *Clinical Psychology: Science and Practice*, 10: 144–156).

Kornfield, J. (2008) *The Wise Heart. Buddhist Psychology for the West*. London: Rider.

Lazar, S. W., Kerr, C. E., Wassermann, R. H., Gray, J., Greve, D. N., and Treadway, M.T., et al. (2005) "Meditation Experience Is Associated with Increased Cortical Thickness." *Neuroreport,* 16, 1893–1897.

Lewis, T., Amini, F., and Lannon, R. (2000). *A General Theory of Love*. New York, NY: Random House.

Loy, D. (2000) *Lack and Transcendence: The Problem of Death and Life in Psychotherapy, Existentialism, and Buddhism*. Amherst, NY: Prometheus Books.

Lutz, A., Slagter, H. E., Dunne, J. D., and Davidson, R. J. (2008) "Attention Regulation and Monitoring in Meditation." *Trends in Cognitive Sciences*, 12: 163–169.

Lutz, A., Slagter, H. E., Rawlings, N. B., Francis, A. D., Greischar, L. L., and Davidson, R. J. (2009) "Mental Training Enhances Attentional Stability: Neural and Behavioral Evidence. *The Journal of Neuroscience*, 29: 13418–13427.

McCullough, M., Tsang, J., and Emmons, R. (2004) "Gratitude in Intermediate Affective Terrain: Links of Gratitude Moods to Individual Differences and Daily Emotional Experience." *Journal of Personality and Social Psychology*, 86: 295–309.

Miller, J. P. (2006) *Educating for Wisdom and Compassion: Creating Conditions for Timeless Learning.* Thousand Oaks, CA: Corwin Press.

Napoli, M., Krech, P. R., and Holley, L. C. (2005) "Mindfulness Training for Elementary School Students: The Attention Academy." *Journal of Applied School Psychology*, 21: 99-125.

Nhat Hanh, Thich (1988) *The Heart of Understanding: Commentaries on the Prajnaparamita Heart Sutra.* Berkeley, CA: Parallax Press.

Nhat Hanh, Thich (1992) *The Diamond that Cuts through Illusion: Commentaries on the Prajnaparamita Diamond Sutra.* Berkeley, CA: Parallax Press.

Nhat Hanh, Thich (1992) *Peace Is Every Step: The Path of Mindfulness in Everyday Life.* New York, NY: Bantam.

Nhat Hanh, Thich (1999) *The Heart of the Buddha's Teaching: Transforming Suffering into Peace, Joy, and Liberation.* New York, NY: Broadway Books.

Nhat Hanh, Thich (2002) *Anger: Wisdom for Cooling the Flames.* New York, NY: Riverhead Books.

Nhat Hanh, Thich (2010) *A Pebble for Your Pocket: Mindful Stories for Children and Grown-ups.* Berkeley, CA: Parallax Press.

Niaura, R., Todaro, J. F., Stroud, L., Spiro, A. III, Ward, K. D., and Weiss, S. (2002) "Hostility, the Metabolic Syndrome, and Incident Coronary Heart Disease." *Health Psychology*, 21: 588–593.

Nordenbo, S. E. (2008) *Lærerkompetanser og elevers læring i barnehage og skole: et systematisk review utført for Kunnskapsdepartementet, Oslo.* København: Danmarks Pædagogiske Universitetsforlag.

Payne, J. P. (2010) *Simplicity Parenting: Using the Extraordinary Power of Less to Raise Calmer, Happier, and More Secure Kids.* New York, NY: Ballantine Books.

Petty, R., Fabriger, L., and Wegener, D. (2003) "Emotional Factors in Attitudes and Persuasion." Davidson. R.J., Sherer, K.R., and Goldsmith, H. eds. *Handbook of Affective Sciences.* New York, NY: Oxford University Press, USA.

Rizzolatti, G., Forgassi, L., and Gallese, V. (2002) "Motor and Cognitive Functions of the Ventral Premotor Cortex." *Current Opinion in Neurobiology*, 12: 149–154.

Rizzolatti, C. and Sinigaglia, C. (2008) *Mirrors in the Brain: How Our Minds Share Actions and Emotions.* New York, NY: Oxford University Press, USA.

Rosenberg, L. (2004) *Breath by Breath: The Liberating Practice of Insight Meditation.* Boston, MA: Shambhala Publications.

Rosenthal, R. (2002) "Covert Communications in Classrooms, Clinics, Courtrooms, and Cubicles." *American Psychologist*, 57: 839–849.

Rotne, N. F. (2007) *Mindfulness. En teoretisk undersøgelse af mindfulness som stresshåndteringsmetode.* Specialeafhandling, Danmarks Pædagogiske Universitet, Aarhus Universitet.

Saltzman, A. and Goldin, P. (2008) "Mindfulness-Based Stress Reduction for School-Age Children. In S. C. Hayes and L. A. Greco, eds. *Acceptance and Mindfulness Treatments for Children and Adolescents.* Oakland, CA: Context Press/New Harbinger. 139–161.

Schein, E. H. (2010) *Organizational Culture and Leadership.* Hoboken, NJ: Jossey-Bass.

Segal, S. V., Teasdale, J. D., and Williams, M. G. (2004) "Mindfulness-Based Cognitive Therapy. Theoretical Rationale and Empirical Status." Hayes, S. C. et al. (2004) *Mindfulness and Acceptance.* New York, NY: Guilford Press.

Segal, Z. V., Williams, J. M. G., and Teasdale, J. D. (2002) *Mindfulness-Based Cognitive Therapy for Depression: A New Approach to Preventing Relapse.* New York, NY: Guilford Press.

Servan-Schreiber, D. (2004) *The Instinct to Heal: Curing Stress, Anxiety, and Depression Without Drugs and Without Talk Therapy.* Emmaus, PA: Rodale Books.

Shapiro, D. H. (1992) "A Preliminary Study of Long-Term Meditators: Goals, Effects, Religious Orientation, Cognitions." *Journal of Transpersonal Psychology*, 24: 23-39.

Shapiro, S. L., and Carlson, L. E. (2009) *The Art and Science of Mindfulness: Integrating Mindfulness into Psychology and the Helping Professions.* Washington, DC: American Psychological Association.

Siegel, D. J. (2007) *The Mindful Brain: Reflection and Attunement in the Cultivation of Well-Being.* New York, NY: W.W. Norton.

Smallwood, J., Fishman, D. J., and Schooler, J. W. (2007) "Counting the Cost of an Absent Mind: Mind Wandering as an Underrecoginzed Influence on Education Performance." *Psychomimic Bulletin & Reviews*, 14: 230–236.

Solloway, S. G. (1999) "Teachers as Contemplative Practitioners: Presence, Meditation, and Mindfulness as a Classroom Practice." Ph.D. http://e-archive.library.okstate.edu/dissertations/AAI9947746

Teasdale, J. D. (1999) "Metacognition, Mindfulness and the Modification of Mood Disorders." *Clinical Psychology and Psychotherapy*, 6: 146–155.

Umiltá, M. A., Kohler, E., Gallese, V., Forgassi, L., Fadiga, L., Keysers, C., and Rizzolatti, G. (2001) "I Know What You Are Doing: A Neurophysiological Study." *Neuron*, 31: 155–165.

Wager, N., Fieldman, G., and Hussey, T. (2003) "The Effect on Ambulatory Blood Pressure of Working under Favourably and Unfavourably Percieved Supervisors." *Occupational Environmental Medicine*, 60: 468–474.

Weissberg, R. P., Durlak, J. A., Taylor, R. D., Dynmicki, A. B., and O'Brien, M. U. (2011) "Promoting Social and Emotional Learning Enhances School Success: Implications of a Meta-Analysis." *Child Development*, 82 (1), 405–432.

Westergaard-Poulsen, P., van Beek, Skewes, J., Bjarkam, C. R., Stubberup, M., Bertelsen, J. (2009). "Long-Term Meditation Is Associated with Increased Gray Matter Density in the Brain Stem." *Neuroport*, 20: 170–174.

Willard, C. (2010). *Child's Mind: Mindfulness Practices to Help Our Children Be More Focused, Calm, and Relaxed.* Berkeley, CA: Parallax Press.

Zillmann, D. (1993). "Mental Control of Angry Aggression." Wegner, D. and Pennebaker, P., eds. *Handbook of Mental Control.* Eaglewood Cliffs, NJ: Prentice Hall.

Related Titles from Parallax Press

Anh's Anger *Gail Silver*

Be Free Where You Are *Thich Nhat Hanh*

Being Peace *Thich Nhat Hanh*

Breathe, You Are Alive! *Thich Nhat Hanh*

Child's Mind *Christopher Willard*

A Handful of Quiet *Thich Nhat Hanh*

The Long Road Turns to Joy *Thich Nhat Hanh*

Mindful Movements *Thich Nhat Hanh*

A Pebble for Your Pocket *Thich Nhat Hanh*

Planting Seeds *Thich Nhat Hanh*

Present Moment Wonderful Moment *Thich Nhat Hanh*

Steps and Stones *Gail Silver*

Touching Peace *Thich Nhat Hanh*

Understanding Our Mind *Thich Nhat Hanh*

Monastics and laypeople practice the art of mindful living in the tradition of Thich Nhat Hanh at retreat communities worldwide. To reach any of these communities, or for information about individuals and families joining for a practice period, please contact:

Plum Village
13 Martineau
33580 Dieulivol, France
www.plumvillage.org

Magnolia Grove Monastery
123 Towles Rd.
Batesville, MS 38606
www.magnoliagrovemonastery.org

Blue Cliff Monastery
3 Mindfulness Road
Pine Bush, NY 12566
www.bluecliffmonastery.org

Deer Park Monastery
2499 Melru Lane
Escondido, CA 92026
www.deerparkmonastery.org

The Mindfulness Bell, a journal of the art of mindful living in the tradition of Thich Nhat Hanh, is published three times a year by Plum Village. To subscribe or to see the worldwide directory of Sanghas, visit www.mindfulnessbell.org

**PARALLAX
PRESS**

Parallax Press, a nonprofit organization,
publishes books on engaged Buddhism
and the practice of mindfulness
by Thich Nhat Hanh and other authors.
For a copy of the catalog, please contact:

Parallax Press
P.O. Box 7355
Berkeley, CA 94707
Tel: (510) 525-0101
www.parallax.org